Cycling in Cyberspace

**Finding Bicycle-Related Information
Through Online Services and the Internet**

Michelle Kienholz

and

Robert Pawlak, Ph.D.

Bicycle Books — San Francisco

Published by:
Bicycle Books, Inc.
1282 - 7th Avenue
San Francisco, CA 94122
USA

Distributed to the book trade by:
USA: National Book Network, Lanham, MD
Canada: Raincoast Book Distribution, Vancouver, BC
UK: Chris Lloyd Sales and Marketing Services, Poole, Dorset

Cover: Kent Lytle, Lytle Design, Alameda, CA
Book design: Michelle L. Kienholz, Montross, VA
Back photo: David S. Cooper, Montross, VA

Publisher's Cataloging in Publication Data
Kienholz, Michelle.
   Cycling in cyberspace : finding bicycle-related information through online services and the internet / Michelle Kienholz and Robert Pawlak.
   p. cm.
   LCCN: 95-83336
   ISBN 0-933201-75-3

   1. Cycling—Directories. 2. Computer bulletin boards—Directories.
3. Internet (Computer networks)   I. Pawlak, Robert.
II. Title.

GV1041.K54 1996   796.6'025
                                   QBI96-20001

To Baba

A Big Thank-You to Online Cyclists

As cyclists living in a rural area, we have long relied on the online bicycle community for information, advice, and support. It is impossible to say "thank you" too many times to the dedicated individuals who maintain the sites described in this book (and hundreds more that we couldn't squeeze in— but you'll find them on your own). Without their efforts, this book wouldn't be possible. You'll "meet" some of these cybercyclists through their comments, advice, and stories in the chapters that follow.

Please remember that every site reviewed in the book is copyrighted by the owner and that no text or images from any online cycling resource should be reprinted or duplicated online without the owner's knowledge or permission. We are especially grateful to the following individuals who allowed us to use images from their sites (listed in order of appearance):

Kathy Johnson, America Online, Inc. (©1995 America Online; Used by Permission)

Stephen King, Tech Tips

Greg Franks, Team Internet

Brent Soderberg, The Virtual Breakaway (©1995 Brent Soderberg)

Patrick Goebel, VeloNet

Scott Rose & Pascal Balthrop, Bicycling Community Page

Carl Flansbaum, Cyber Cyclery

Diane Greer, Great Outdoors Recreational Pages (GORP) (All Original Material and HTML Coding on GORP is © 1994, 1995 by Greer Consulting Services, Inc. All Rights Reserved)

Susan Mernit & Newhouse New Media, US Bicycling Hall of Fame

Dan Swofford & WebSmith, VeloLinQ

Ray Schumacher, Cool Places to Ride

Chris Johnston, Fat Tire Wire

Lindsay Marshall, The Mountain Bike Pages

Ross Findlayson, Mountain Biking (©1995 Ross Findlayson; Title Graphic ©1995 David Le)

Geff Hinds, MuDSLuTs

Hadley Taylor, WOMBATS (©1995 WOMBATS)

Scott B. Roat, Worldguide

Matt Lanning, Fat Tire Fotos

Séamus Shortall, Irish Cycling Page

Colleen Doody & Chris McKenney, Team Working Title

Gilbert Cattoire, World Media

Karl Anderson, C.H.U.N.K. 666

Michael Hessey & Nigel Sadler, Moulton Bicycle

Wade Blomgren, Tandem Page (tandem@hobbes logo created by Ann Summers, Jim Becker, et al.)

Randy Swart, Bicycle Helmet Safety Institute (artwork, ©1995 Nancy Jennis Olds)

Peter Hickey, Winter Cycling

Philip Graitcer, Snell Memorial Foundation

Steve Howard, Big Ring the Zine (©1995 Steven Howard)

Maurice Tierney, Dirt Rag

David Schloss, GearHead Magazine

Dan Koeppel, MBElectro

Greg Shepherd, Tandem Magazine

Chuck Rucker, Triathlete Online, Winning Magazine Online

Jeff Rogers, Endurance Training Journal

Thomas Burhkolder, UCSD Neuromuscular Physiology Laboratory

Aaron Bromagem, Yahoo! Corporation

Paul Wilson, PB's Triathlon Home Page

Jason MacDonald, Triathlon & Cycling

Charles Hofacker, The Big Ring

Tim Stewart, The Cycle Center: The Big Index

Mike Olfe, Lycos, Inc.: The Catalog of the Internet

May Liang, America Online, Inc., WebCrawler (©1995 American Online, Inc. All Rights Reserved)

Bryn Dole, The WWW Bicycle Lane (© 1995 Bryn Dole)

Ken Manning & Mike Taffe, WWW Cycling Links (©1995 Ken Manning & Mike Taffe)

Table of Contents

Chapter 1

Using a Bulletin Board System

The bulletin board system (BBS) is the most basic online link. You only need a computer and a modem to use a BBS. The BBS itself is a computer with special software that allows other computers to connect to it. A BBS may be someone's personal computer at home or a dedicated machine in an office.

You can use a BBS to read messages left by other people, to write your own comments or questions, to "chat" with other cyclists through your keyboard, to check ride schedules and weather forecasts, or to download (copy from the BBS to your computer) trail maps. Some BBSs also allow you to send and receive Internet e-mail and to read Usenet newsgroups (Chapter 3). Help is usually available online from friendly system operators (sysops). Best of all, most BBSs are free or charge a small annual fee for full access.

We've listed a few BBSs with cycling resources in Appendix B. To find a BBS in your calling area, check in local computer papers, *Computer Shopper, Boardwatch Magazine*, or ask at a computer store. America Online offers a BBS database that you can search by keyword, such as "cycling" or "bicycle." Most commercial services offer help in finding a local BBS.

The easiest way to learn about BBSs is to tour one. The Rochester Bicycling Club BBS is a friendly place to learn about getting online and is a model for how other bike clubs could provide this type of convenient service for their members. (If this tour, which is representative of most BBSs, is confusing, try the even simpler Bicycle Bulletin Board at 619-720-1830.)

Signing On

You probably received some communications software with your modem or computer that allows you to dial up other computers. Sometimes this software is called a "terminal" program. Launch the program and look for the command or icon that allows you to type in a phone number to dial (probably "Dial" or "Connect" or a telephone icon).

Now type in 1-716-265-3357 (the Rochester Bicycling Club BBS). Your software should allow you to save the information so that you don't have to retype the same number, but for now just concentrate on signing on.

You will hear the modem dialing the phone, then some static-like noise, and then a series of trills and beeps as the modems talk to each other. Eventually you will see something like the following message:

```
ATDT1-716-265-3357
CONNECT 57600
        ::: Connect 14400 To rbcbbs - Node # 1 3903 :::
PowerBBS(tm) (1 line) v 4.01 (c) 1989-1995 PowerBBS
```

```
Computing
Node #1;  Locked in at 19200 bps
Your Administrator is TODD CALVIN
ANSI Detected!
Try PowerAccess for a GUI interface!

PowerAccess for Windows will allow you to enjoy a full
multimedia experience when calling this BBS! It also
supports ASCII/ANSI with X/Y/Zmodem protocols! (1415 k)
18.7 mins
Download PowerAccess Terminal Package (Y=Yes,N=No)?
[ENTER=No]: No


* * * * * * * * * * * * * * * * * * * * * * * * * * * * * * * * * * * * *
*                                                     *
*            W E L C O M E    T O                     *
*         Rochester Bicycling Club BBS                *
*         running at 300 to 14.4K  baud               *
*                    ---                              *
*         League of American Bicyclists               *
*    International Mountain Bicycle Assoc              *
*  Friends of the Genesee Valley Greenway             *
*                                                     *
* * * * * * * * * * * * * * * * * * * * * * * * * * * * * * * * * * * * *
```

When you see the opening lines of seeming gibberish, just ignore them.
When in doubt, hit the <Enter> or <Return> or <ESC> key. The
PowerAccess "GUI interface" is a Windows or Macintosh-like graphical
interface that makes using the BBS easier, but it is not essential.

After the welcome message, you will be asked for your name, address, and
other information. Some questions are about your monitor and computer-
related controls. This is to make sure the BBS "looks" right on your computer. Two common terminal protocols, VT100 and ANSI BBS, are available
in most communications software. You could select either of these or just use
the default settings by hitting <Return>. Don't worry too much about
selecting the wrong settings. You can always change them later or hang up
and sign on again to start from scratch. These settings do *not* affect the
operation of your own computer. They determine how the BBS screens will
appear on your monitor and how you retrieve files from the BBS. Not all
BBSs request this information, and some, like the Rochester Bicycling Club
BBS, offer their own graphical interface to make it easier for you to sign on.

If you haven't gotten this far, try turning your modem off and back on
again and check to ensure that the communication settings are as follows:

• data bits = 8
• parity = none
• stop bits = 1

These are the most common modem settings. You may also want to match your modem speed with the BBS (in this case, anywhere from 300 baud to 14,400 baud). If all this fails, you might have a port conflict, a computer configuration problem, or a modem initialization problem, in which case you may need to call for technical support (or a good computer-savvy friend).

Getting back to the sign-on procedure, one important piece of information you will be asked to provide is a password. When you sign on again, you will only be asked for your name and password, which will uniquely identify you to the BBS. You shouldn't use any part of your name or address or any common words for a password. A mixture of letters and numbers is often best. However, you also shouldn't make the password so difficult that you can't remember it. No matter what password you choose, write it down with the name of the BBS (if you use more than one BBS, use different passwords). It's also a good idea to update (change) your password occasionally.

What's Available?

Each BBS is different in terms of what it offers. The BBS will often first ask you if you want to read a newsletter or bulletin before going to the main menu. These documents tell you about new features and planned enhancements. On a cycling BBS, they may also include ride schedules, club news, and other timely information. If you opt to skip them at this point of the sign-on procedure, you can go back and read them later from the main menu of the BBS.

The most important sections of the BBS are the message and the file areas. The message area is where you can exchange information, advice, and encouragement with other cyclists by writing short notes. When you first sign on, the BBS checks to see if anyone has sent you an e-mail message (see Chapter 3) or responded to a note that you posted on a message board. You will probably find local message groups that discuss issues of regional interest. If the BBS offers Usenet newsgroups (also in Chapter 3), you will have an international online forum to join. The file area is where the BBS stores text, graphics, and software for public use. You'll find everything from helmet information to mountain bike trail maps to spoke length calculators.

Some BBSs offer conference areas where you can "chat" (through your keyboard) with other people in real time. Sometimes "meetings" are scheduled with a moderator presiding and perhaps a guest expert lending his or her expertise. Otherwise, you can arrange to meet cross-country cycling aficionados online to discuss the latest news and to share experiences. Many BBSs also offer you the opportunity to send and receive e-mail over the Internet, though you'll likely pay a nominal annual fee for this service. You'll find games, questionnaires, computer assistance, classified ads, and many other interesting features as you explore various BBSs.

Navigating the File Area

Getting back to the Rochester Bicycling Club BBS, let's go to the file areas. When you begin using any new BBS, you'll want to see what's available with the List option. In the Rochester BBS, you'll find the following choices (please note that some names have been shortened throughout this chapter, and the BBS has no doubt been updated since we published the book):

```
[Q]uit, [N]ext, Enter areas [1..26], [U]pload, [L]ist,
[A]ll: [ENTER=ALL]: L

Rochester Bicycling Club File areas

1.  Bicycle Related Software
============================================================
2.  Common RBC Files              12. Windows apps
3.  Board Data Bases              13. Windows utilities
4.  New York Bicycle Coalition    14. Windows fonts
5.  International Mtn Bike Asso    15. Windows games
6.  Newsletter Submissions        16. Windows bitmaps
7.  Old Newsletter Articles       17. Windows graphics
8.  Restricted Area               18. Windows icons
9.  Communication Utilities       19. DOS business apps
10. RBC Mapset (by Map#)          20. DOS shareware
11. Bicycle artwork               21. DOS education
23. Genesee Valley Greenway       22. DOS entertainment
============================================================
26. Recent Uploads
============================================================
24. PowerBBS Shareware
25. System Bulletins
```

As you can see, each area is fairly self-explanatory. So are your options for viewing the individual files. You can search for a particular file or subject, view only those files added after a certain date, or scan through the entire list.

```
        ** FILE MENU **

[D].......Download a File(s)    [Q]..........Utilities Menu
[U].........Upload a File(s)    [M].......Message/Mail Menu
[L].....List available Files
[H]....................Help
[N].....New Files since last    [G]........Goodbye & Log Off
[S].........Search File List

==== file menu utilities ===
[P]....Set Download Protocol
```

If you're not from New York or the Rochester area, you'll probably want to
List the files in the Bicycle Related Software area (file area 1).

```
[D]ownload, [return] exit, Area(s) to list [1..26], [L]ist,
[M]ark? 1
Display a short file listing (with a max of 2 description
lines) [ENTER=Yes]:Yes
========================================================================
Filename      Size    Date      Description
========================================================================

A 21CCLOG.ZIP 334257 01-26-95 Bicycle training software (DOS)

B BIKE20.ZIP   80630 01-19-95  Windows program that allows you
                               to track your rides

C GEAR.ZIP     10897 12-04-92  Simple gear chart for DOS

D NTSV10.ZIP   88328 02-16-95  Nutrition tracking system (DOS)

E SPOKE.C       1024 10-14-93   C-Source code for spoke calc

F SPOKEW11.EXE 239109 10-13-93 Spoke Calculator for Windows

G TRAIN.ZIP     81819 12-04-92  Personal training log (DOS)

H WGEARCHT.ZIP 218275 10-03-93 Windows Gear Charter v1.3

[D]ownload, [return] exit, Area(s) to list [1..26], [L]ist,
[M]ark?
```

You may already know that files ending in .exe are uncompressed or self-extracting executable files (software), and that files ending in .zip are compressed software that require PKZip to "unzip" them. While the files on this BBS are all designed to run under DOS or Windows, many BBSs do include Macintosh software, and the text and graphics files can be opened using almost any computer configuration.

Suppose you'd like to check the training log (BIKE20.ZIP). You must have PKZip or similar shareware and, just as important, you must have shareware or software built into your operating system to check for viruses. Executable files and macros (automated command sequences) must all be checked for viruses. Text and graphic files are impossible to infect and are a safer bet if you don't want to risk a computer virus. If you plan to use BBSs and download software frequently, be sure to back up your hard drive, at least the critical files, before launching any downloaded software.

If you see several files that you'd like to download, you can Mark them (for retrieval) so they are downloaded from the BBS to your computer all at once. In our example, though, you'll just download the training log. When you opt to Download, you are given the following choices:

```
[D]ownload, [return] exit, Area(s) to list [1..26], [L]ist,
[M]ark? D

Press [RETURN]:

        [Y] Ymodem Batch
        [G] YmodemG Batch
        [X] Xmodem/XmodemCRC
        [K] modem-1K
        [E] modem-1KG
        [Z] Zmodem
        [o] DAT| sz

Select which protocol, [N=None], [ENTER=N]? Z
```

Which method you choose to download the file (transferring it from the BBS to your computer) will depend on your communications software. However, most programs support Zmodem, which is generally fast and trouble-free and also allows you to resume the file transfer if your call is interrupted. Some BBSs point out that Zmodem is the best choice.

Once you've selected a protocol, the BBS estimates the amount of time it will take to download the file and confirms the settings you have selected. You'll be given the option of logging off the service after the transfer is complete. This is convenient if the file is large (or you're downloading several files) and you have better things to do with your time than watch a bar graph show the status of the transfer.

```
Filename(s)/Wildcards to Download (Max=39, K=9999,
Time=196) ==> BIKE20.ZIP
Searching directories.  Please wait...

 BIKE20.ZIP  (  79 k)      Est Time:    1.1mins

Total Byte Count:  80630
  Estimated Time:  1.1 mins
        Protocol:  Z (Zmodem)
         File(s):  BIKE20.ZIP

Transfer Option: (A)bort, (B)egin, (L)ogoff when done,
[ENTER=B]: B
```

```
Begin your transfer mode; Repeat Ctrl-X to abort

**B00000000000000

Transfer completed (1 files [78 k] at 831.0 cps.
Downloaded [BIKE20.ZIP] at 831 CPS using (Z).
```

Now you have the compressed training log on your hard drive. You'll need to unzip it, check it for viruses, and see if there is a shareware fee. But before signing off to do this, you'll want to check the message areas first.

Reading the Message Area

The message area of any BBS includes both local and global discussion groups, usually organized by topic. When first using a BBS, you will often find yourself in a general or local message area, which is for local BBS users to exchange messages. Unless you live nearby, you probably won't find these notes useful. You'll instead want to join a discussion group that focuses on a particular type of cycling, such as road racing, repair, touring, or mountain biking. As with the file areas, you can list and switch among message areas quite easily.

```
    Message area: ** General Messages **

  --Message Options--
[S]..Scan Messages                  [M]..Users Search/List
[A]..List/Change Msg Area
[R]..Read Message                   [L]..Last Message Read
[C]..Comment to Sysop
[E]..Enter Message                  [U]..Areas to Scan
[D]..Download Messages

You're viewing General Messages Press (A) to list or change
message area

Mail Menu Command? A

Please Select a New Message Forum

0. General Messages (local)
1. Buy/Sell Trade Area (local)
2. Internet Mail Gateway * (net)
3. rec.bicycles.rides newsgroup (net)
4. rec.bicycles.soc newsgroup (net)
5. rec.bicycles.misc newsgroup (net)
6. rec.bicycles.racing newsgroup (net)
7. rec.bicycles.tech newsgroup (net)
8. rec.bicycles.offroad (net)
```

Suppose you decide to check the messages on rec.bicycles.offroad (a Usenet newsgroup for mountain bikers). You will be given the following options:

```
Welcome MICHELLE, you have joined the following Message area:
INTNN BICYCLES.OFFRO

Messages Available :   309
 Low message number:   1
High message number:   309
  Last Message read:   0


Press [RETURN]:

[?]Help [A]rea [D]el [N]ext Forum [R]eply [S]earch [Y]ours
# 0 [1..309] [Q]uit, [L]ist Commands [ENTER=1+]: L
```

You can `List` the available commands to see how you can read through the 309 messages most efficiently (the [Y]ours refers to any messages on the newsgroup addressed to you personally). If you are looking for information on a particular topic—suppose you're considering a new Specialized bike— you will probably want to `Search` through messages. You can also look for messages from a particular person or posted on a certain day or days. The other commands refer to ways to mark individual messages, depending on whether you want to be able to read them later or send them to a friend.

```
Read Menu

Y)OUR MAIL              C)opy message
A)rea change            S)earch through messages
H)elp                   N)ext message FORUM
D)elete message         O)riginal message
P)rotect message        E)dit message
M)ove message           U)nprotect message
R)eply to message       Q)uit reading
B)ring back message   For(W)ard message

+)Forward read          -)Reverse read

[?]Help [A]rea [D]el [N]ext Forum [R]eply [S]earch [Y]ours
# 0 [1..309] [Q]uit, [L]ist Commands [ENTER=1+]: S
Enter text to scan, [ENTER]=Quit

(&) = And, (|) = Or, (*) or (?) = Wildcard
 |---+---1---+---2---+---3---+---4---+---5|
? Specialized

Enter message # to begin scanning: [ENTER=1+]:
```

At this point, the BBS will stop at each message in which the word "Specialized" is used in any context. Some messages may be from people seeking or giving advice about a particular bicycle, component, or accessory (such as shoes). Some messages may be using the word "specialized" in a more generic sense. Each message is identified by its unique number and shows the date and time it was posted, the author's name and e-mail address, the subject or topic of the message, and to whom the message is addressed (for example, on local message boards, one person or a group can be named).

The options for reading and writing messages are just as straightforward. You can scan through the messages quickly (author and topic line) and mark individual notes to read later, or read through them all sequentially. You can either respond to an existing message or post your own new message. You'll get the hang of participating in discussions when you try a BBS yourself.

Software is also available for you to download messages from specific discussion groups and to upload messages that you compose offline. This type of program (often a QWK utility) allows you to sign on and off very quickly, which will reduce your long-distance charges and online time.

When you're ready to sign off, just type G or Goodbye on most BBSs to log off and hang up. The main menu will show the proper command. If you're really desperate, you can turn off your modem. Then you should scroll back through the text file of your online session so you can write down the important commands and become more familiar with the BBS. You may even want to save this text or capture the entire session to a text file (you'll need to set this up before you sign on), if your communications software supports this option. If you have questions about using any BBS menus, you are best off sending a message to the sysop for help when you next sign on.

It's funny how things develop, and the implementation of a BBS system just happened. Our club was host to the 1993 Great Eastern Rally in Geneseo, New York. It was a large task to complete, and coordination between our committee was well served by setting up a private computer BBS to centralize information and materials as well as to keep in touch. It provided the necessary hub of communications. After completing the rally, we decided to make the board public as an experiment. I added appropriate materials and information, added Internet mail and news, and posted the phone number. As word spread, the system became well utilized, and we currently have over 300 users. The addition of a Web site and Internet mailing list allows us to get information out to users of all systems. I recommend it for any club.

Todd Calvin, System Administrator, Rochester Bicycle Club BBS

A Word About Freenets

If you're very fortunate, you live in an area served by a freenet. A freenet has the local flavor and friendliness of a BBS but offers much more. Freenets are often called electronic villages, and you might think of them as a combination town hall and community center. When you sign on, you'll find the menus organized by building or civic group (rather than by message area or file area). You'll find political and social news, library offerings, health clinics, discussion groups, weather reports, and many other issues of local interest. However, freenets may also connect the town with the rest of the world through the Internet.

Cleveland, Ohio, is home to the National Public Telecomputing Network (NPTN), an organization working to make computer networking services available to everyone, and several cities in Ohio maintain freenets. For the latest details on freenets worldwide, dial 1-216-247-6196 with your modem (login Visitor when you are asked for this information). Go through the menus to get to NPTN Special Projects, About the NPTN, and NPTN Affiliates and Organizing Committees. If the NPTN BBS has been reorganized since this book was published, try similar-sounding directory names or check in a general reference book about BBSs or the Internet.

Because they are free (or almost free—most are supported by donations and minimal user fees), freenets are extremely busy and can be hard to sign on to. You may be tempted to use a freenet in another city to get to the Internet, but you'll probably be frustrated by busy signals, and you'll be tying up resources meant for people living in that specific geographic area. If you don't have a local university or freenet through which you can maintain an online account, you'll need to try a commercial service (such as America Online, Delphi, or any of the other major services) or an Internet provider (such as Netcom, Pipeline, or another local or regional online access company).

Chapter 2

Cyclists Online on America Online

You can choose from several commercial online services to gain access to wire news, encyclopedias, travel services, games, magazines, newspapers, computer support, and hundreds of forums and special interest groups. Commercial services are generally faster and easier to use than BBSs. Most use a graphical interface, while some also offer a text interface, which is useful for disabled individuals and anyone with a slow modem or older computer.

Unlike many BBSs, commercial services charge subscription fees. Some services offer a monthly fee with a per-hour online charge. Other services have more complicated pricing structures. Most offer a free trial period that allows you to see what's available and at what cost. If you're not familiar with a particular service, you should take advantage of the free trial membership to explore it. If you live in an urban area, the service will probably have a local phone number for you to use. Some have toll-free numbers, but these are not always less expensive than dialing long distance to another state.

Cyclists will find useful information on any commercial service. Most offer a general cycling discussion group as part of a larger sports or outdoors forum. On CompuServe (800-848-8990), for example, you would spend your time in the Outdoors Activities Forum, while on eWorld (800-775-4556), you'd head for Energy Express and the Health Club. On Prodigy (800-776-3449), you'll find a few documents in the Keeping Fit area. GEnie (800-638-9636) offers Adventure Atlas, which may offer some help in planning your next cycling tour, and a Sports RoundTable. On Delphi (800-695-4005), you could start your own custom cycling forum. However, America Online is the best all-around choice in terms of the resources available for cyclists.

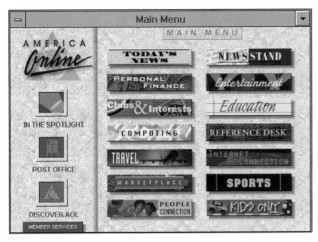

America Online's main menu lets you point and click to move through the service. Most cycling resources are available under Newsstand, Clubs & Interests, and Sports.

America Online (AOL) software is compatible with the Macintosh, Windows, and DOS operating systems. You can use either keyboard commands or a mouse to navigate through the service. Most of the cycling-related material is in the Clubs & Interests section, where you'll find Bicycling Magazine Online and BikeNet. Many, many bicycle-related companies maintain AOL accounts, as you'll note from the e-mail addresses in Appendix E. Of course, as do all of the commercial services, AOL also provides Internet access, which is described in Chapter 3.

Finally, don't let the name fool you. Anyone in the world with a computer, a modem, and a working phone line can use AOL. Access numbers are available in Australia, Austria, Belarus, Belgium, Bulgaria, Canada, Colombia, Denmark, Estonia, Finland, France, Germany, Greece, Hong Kong, Hungary, Indonesia, Ireland, Israel, Italy, Japan, Kazakhstan, Korea, Kuwait, Latvia, Lithuania, Luxembourg, Mexico, the Netherlands, New Zealand, Norway, Peru, the Philippines, Portugal, Romania, Russia, Singapore, Spain, Sweden, Switzerland, Taiwan, Ukraine, the United Kingdom, Uzebekistan, and Venezuela (additional local numbers will be available as more SprintNet Access Centers come online). In the United States, call 800-827-6364 to request the free software; outside the U.S., call 703-318-7740.

The two most important areas on AOL (for cyclists, that is) are Bicycling Magazine Online and BikeNet. Having access to these resources alone is worth the subscription, particularly if you're new to online services and aren't ready to jump straight into the Internet on your own. Although dozens of excellent, well-organized resources are available on the Internet, the individuals maintaining these sites usually aren't being paid for their services and do have their own personal lives. Bicycling Magazine Online and BikeNet can be counted on to provide consistent, quality information and assistance.

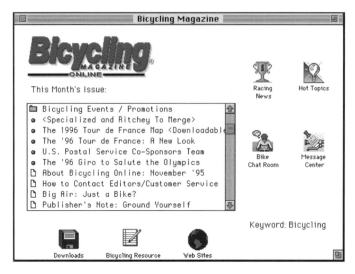

Bicycling Magazine Online includes articles and columns from the print magazine, plus late-breaking news, cycling resources, and discussion groups.

Bicycling Magazine Online

Directions: Use the keyword Bicycling (under the Go To or Go To Keyword menu) *or* click on Clubs & Interests *or* on Newsstand

You might expect to find a few teaser articles and information about sub-scribing (in fact, you can use an online form to subscribe), but you'll prob-ably be overwhelmed at the range and depth of resources offered here. Rodale Press staff members manage this impressive forum, which includes many of the articles (some are longer than the printed versions since space and paper costs aren't problems) from Bicycling Magazine and some from Mountain Bike Magazine, plus a sponsor showcase, race coverage, the Bicycling Tour Guide, special events, guest speakers in the auditorium, and much more. You can send e-mail to DWBicMag@aol.com.

Sponsor Showcase

The Sponsor Showcase features useful information aside from specs and price sheets, such as details about Polar Heart Rate Seminars and the Bicycle Utah Vacation Guide. The Bicycling Tour Guide gives you basic touring tips plus detailed reviews and logistics for outstanding tours around the world. You

Bicycling Online is the digital companion to the print Bicycling Maga-zine, the world's number one road and mountain biking publication. Bicycling Online uses the speed of the medium by providing original same-day race stories and results from events such as the Tour de France and the Tour DuPont. Bicycling Online is also one of the few sources for same-day, original stories and results from major mountain bike events, such as NORBA nationals and the Grundig World Cup series. Bicycling Online hires professional freelance photographers such as Rich Etchberger and Graham Watson to provide exceptional images for its downloads area. Also available under its downloads icon are dozens of shareware training, gear charting, and other programs. Bicycling Online maintains a sampling of current-issue stories from the print Bicycling, but supple-ments this with breaking news from the industry and consumer realms. A dozen well-used message centers—focusing on everything from technical chatter to a women's center, plus the popular "Ask the Factory Reps," with more than 75 companies—provide users with the opportunity to interact with the industry and fellow riders. A live chat room and virtual audito-riums may host VIP guests.
Fred Zahradnik

can monitor the Bicycling Events/Promotions folder for contest announcements, special chat room guests, National MS Society Bike Tours, and
Century Challenge Rides. Sometimes Bicycling sponsors cyberconferences,
complete with polls, editorials, online discussions, guest speakers, and an
executive summary (archives of live online discussions available for reading).

Racing News

If you don't like waiting until midnight for a five-minute blip about bike
racing, make the Racing News trophy cup your first stop. Bicycling Magazine
Online posts daily updates for all major road and mountain bike races
around the world, including text and photographs. Sometimes a rider in the
race will provide personal reflections on the day's events, and the top ten
standings are always listed. During the Tour de France, Bicycling sets up a
special section with links to Reuters' wire stories, Bicycling summaries,
television schedules, photographs, stage information and maps, and more.

Hot Topics

If you'd like to check the resources used to develop magazine articles, turn on
the Hot Topics light bulb. The editors have stocked each topic area with
"digital booklets," articles from back issues, question and answer columns,
and special reports. The Hot Topics area is divided into:
• Training, Fitness, and Nutrition (training for real people)
• Tech Zone (product reviews, bicycle tests, answers to tech questions)
• Women's Cycling
• New Cyclist/Beginner Assistance (getting started)

Bicycling Online's Racing News offers the latest stories and photos.

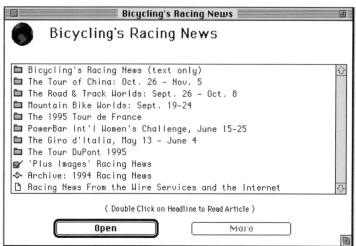

```
------  __o
------ _`\<,_
---- (*)/(*)
```

Bike Chat Room

A shared resource between Bicycling Magazine Online and BikeNet, the Bike Chat Room is open for conversation 24 hours a day, 7 days a week. Rodale Press schedules regular featured chats in the larger AOL auditoriums, where a moderator receives questions from the audience, and the guest speaker responds in real time. It's like a call-in radio show, only you see rather than hear the questions and answers. The transcripts of these special sessions are usually archived and available for reading online or downloading as a text file.

Message Center

Here's where you can ask the editors of Bicycling Magazine and Mountain Bike Magazine those questions that never made it to print before and voice your opinions on individual articles or the overall style of the magazine. Cycling industry representatives are also available to offer very customized customer support. In the Ask the Factory Reps categories (A-L and M-Z), you'll receive help from representatives at more than 70 companies from Avocet to Vetta. This is also where cyclists exchange news, advice, and comments. Message Center categories include:

- General/News (recumbents, commuting, duathlons, hybrids, etc.)
- Technical/Component Chatter (Campy versus Shimano never dies)
- Training, Fitness, & Nutrition (will those supplements really help?)
- Road and Mountain Bike Racing (citizen, masters, amateur, pro)
- Touring, Travel, & Vacations (Arizona to Australia)
- Women's Cycling Topics (lots on saddles, clothes, frames, and kids)

Some of the most valuable topics in each category are the question and answer folders, such as Ask the Coach (Roger Young) or Ask the Therapist (Randy Ice, P.T., C.C.S.). Where else could you talk to Roger Young about your time trial form?

Downloads

The Bicycling Magazine Online software and text libraries are full of useful files that you'll want on your own hard drive. In the Bicycling Software library, you can download survey results, specialty source lists, injury prevention and treatment tips, a full index to the previous year of Bicycling Magazine, and other focused cycling topics. Bicycling Images has photographs of racers (mountain and road), components, and bikes, as well as race course maps. Cycling Shareware & Images includes software (training logs, databases, gear and spoke length calculators, screen art, and more) and graphic files, such as three-dimensional topographical maps from the U.S. Geological Survey. If you need a computer program to view photographs, you can turn to the GIF Viewers library, which includes software for DOS, Windows, and Macintosh. For help with bike components, check the Product Information Center.

BikeNet: The Bicycle Network

Directions: Use the keyword BikeNet (under the Go To or Go To Keyword menu) *or* click on Clubs & Interests

BikeNet is just that: a communication network among cyclists. Mountain bikers, road racers, tourists, commuters, and everyone else on two wheels will find a home here. (BikeNet is also a BBS discussion group.) BikeNet was launched by TheCyclist (aka Tim Oey) in August 1992. This volunteer-operated forum is sponsored by the Adventure Cycling Association (formerly Bikecentennial), the Bicycle Federation of America, the International Mountain Biking Association, the League of American Bicyclists, and the United States Cycling Federation. Each of these groups maintains their own forum, where you can read articles, check file libraries, and exchange messages.

If you're new to AOL, you'll find the How to Best Use BikeNet folder especially helpful. You can read details about various BikeNet features and basic instructions for getting to other bicycle-related areas on AOL, such as Bicycling Magazine Online. You can enter the Bike Chat Room whenever you like, but regular meetings are scheduled every night of the week (check online for the latest details). You "chat" live by posting short notes visible to all participants as part of a running dialog. BikeNet meetings are scheduled for women cyclists, bike advocates, mountain bikers, and guest speakers, among others. As noted earlier, Bicycling Magazine Online shares the Bike Chat Room and schedules its own seminars and rap sessions as well.

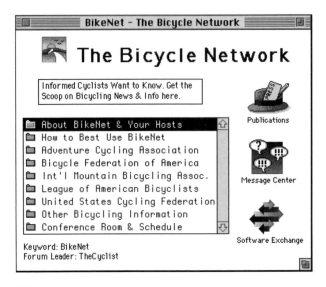

BikeNet serves as a gathering place for many cycling organizations.

Message Center

Electronic message centers allow you to share expertise, ask questions, meet cyclists with similar interests and goals, and buy and sell bicycle equipment. Typing notes on a keyboard may not sound exciting, but message centers are hotbeds of activity on AOL and throughout the Internet. The BikeNet Message Center has a dozen or so categories. If you want to check on a particular category or topic frequently, you can save time by using the Find New or Find Since search tools.

When you open a topic folder, you'll find a long list of messages, starting with the one most recently posted. Topics and messages are identified by their subject line. You can also see when the original message was posted, how many people have responded to the original message, and when the most recent response was posted. This information will help you identify lively discussions and recognize when a topic has been put to rest.

Software Exchange

BikeNet's Software Exchange is where you can give (upload) and receive (download) cycling-related files. BikeNet staff check uploaded files for viruses and other problems before they are made available to the general online public. In the BikeNet General library, you'll find schedules, routes, newsletters, and other useful documents. The BikeNet Graphics library offers pictures meant to instruct, entertain, and customize your computer. BikeNet Text archives chat sessions and documents on common cycling topics in text (ASCII) format, and the Newsletter Exchange allows such organizations as the San Jose Bicycle Club, the Birmingham Bicycle Club, the Illinois Cyclist, and many others to make their publications widely available.

```
┌─────────────────────────────────────────────────────┐
│ ▤▤▤▤▤▤      BikeNet Message Center      ▤▤▤▤▤▤      │
├─────────────────────────────────────────────────────┤
│          Click "list categories" to view all boards, "Find New" to see  │
│          new messages since you last visited, or "Find Since".          │
│                                                                          │
│   Categories: 12              Topics/Postings      Latest                │
│      📁 Regional Trails, Tours & New    50/5451      11/16/95 ▲          │
│      📁 Bikes                           50/2806      11/16/95            │
│      📁 Mountain Bikes                  50/5234      11/16/95            │
│      📁 Bike Components                 47/3098      11/16/95            │
│      📁 Bike Accessories                45/1732      11/15/95            │
│      📁 Bicyclist Training & Fitness    46/914       11/16/95            │
│      📁 Bike Racing                     48/2034      11/16/95            │
│      📁 United States Cycling Federa    50/1604      11/16/95            │
│      📁 Bicycle Organizations           44/833       11/16/95            │
│      📁 Bike Advocacy                   28/1390      11/16/95 ▼          │
│                                                                          │
│      📁              🔍              📇             🅡                   │
│                                                    Help & Info           │
│   List Topics      Find New        Find Since                           │
└─────────────────────────────────────────────────────┘
```

Message Centers in BikeNet and throughout America Online are full of advice, opinions, news, and other useful information.

Publications

You'll find all the various documents available throughout BikeNet in one convenient location. This includes the Rides & Events Calendar, Bike Reference, Bike News from All Over, Bicycle Organizations, and article collections from the sponsoring organizations. If you don't want to dig through several folders to find help with a particular topic, you can search the forum by keyword (such as "commute" or "mountain bike").

Adventure Cycling Association (ACA)

This not-for-profit organization promotes recreational cycling and serves more than 40,000 members. The Adventure Cycling Association offers its members The Cyclists' Yellow Pages, Adventure Cyclist Magazine, guided bicycle tours, map discounts, travel benefits, and free bicycle transport on Northwest Airlines. On BikeNet, the ACA announces tours, describes bike routes, and posts press releases (explaining new routes and maps and how to order them).

Bicycle Federation of America (BFA)

This national nonprofit group promotes the safe use of bicycles as a means of transportation and supports pedestrian advocacy as well. The BFA offers technical assistance, consulting services, referrals, education programs, conferences, training, and a monthly newsletter, Pro Bike News. You can search through the BFA Library, Pro Bike News articles, and all BFA publications available on AOL to find bicycle advocacy information. Included are bicycle-related laws, commuting tips, planning guides for Bike Week and Bike Month, and guidelines for starting a state or local advocacy group.

Adventure Cycling Association (formerly Bikecentennial) offers many valuable resources for touring cyclists.

International Mountain Bicycling Association (IMBA)

This worldwide organization promotes responsible mountain biking and land access for cyclists. IMBA participates in national efforts to establish and maintain trail networks, helps members solve local or regional conflicts, and manages a library of political tactics, scientific studies, land management techniques, and environmental considerations. Their BikeNet presence includes IMBA's Rules of the Trail, information on how to start a mountain bike club, the IMBA Library (with past and current issues of Trail News and other documents), and a collection of IMBA articles. You can search all available documents by keyword.

League of American Bicyclists (LAB)

This member-supported advocacy organization has worked to improve the quality of cycling since 1880. The League represents cyclists' views on bicycle facility funding, road design and maintenance, bridge and trail access, and safety standards. The LAB also maintains an active education program designed to teach children and adults the principles of safe and effective cycling and to help motorists and law enforcement agencies recognize the rights of cyclists on the road. Online you'll find LAB articles, the LAB Library, and several useful documents full of tips and information about LAB programs. Tourists will want to download the complete text of the Long Distance Bicycle Touring Workshop Manual. As usual, the entire forum can be searched by keyword.

The International Mountain Bicycling Association entered cyberspace in 1992 when we helped to form the BikeNet forum on America Online. IMBA leaders communicate with each other constantly through this medium. We monitor and participate in bicycling forums on AOL and Usenet Newsgroups. Thanks to computer modems, we have established contacts as far away as New Zealand. Often these communications end up in our printed bi-monthly newsletter, "IMBA Trail News." We upload text copies of the newsletter to BikeNet and other sites. IMBA established a World Wide Web page during the summer of 1995. Direct your Web browser to http://www.outdoorlink.com/IMBA

IMBA is dedicated to promoting mountain bicycling through environmentally and socially responsible use of land.

Gary Sprung
IMBA Communications Director

United States Cycling Federation (USCF)

The national governing body for amateur bicycle racing in the United States sponsors training camps, trains officials, oversees technical aspects of racing, maintains bicycle safety standards, and works to enhance the popularity of the sport of bicycle racing. Two subsidiary organizations of the USCF, the National Off-Road Bicycling Association (NORBA) and the National Collegiate Cycling Association (NCCA), govern mountain bike racing and college-level racing, respectively. The USCF addresses the needs of everyone from school-age junior riders to Olympic competitors to master level racers. On BikeNet, the USCF offers information about itself and individual race events, resources (cycling records, champions, teams, staff members, and media guides), a Message Board, and a Library (USCF publications, fitness tests, race promotion tips, club sponsorship, and so on).

Other Bicycling Information

BikeNet invites local and regional bicycle organizations to post information about themselves on the Message Center, in a file uploaded to the Library, and/or in a text file stored in the Other Bicycling Information folder. The latter option offers groups the opportunity to provide a membership application online as well. Clubs and organizations can upload text versions of their newsletter and give details as to when and where they meet (offline). Organizations currently represented range from local clubs to state coalitions to national associations, such as the National Bike Registry and Athletes in Action. The Other Bicycling Information area on BikeNet also includes instructions for finding cycling information and resources on the Internet.

BikeNet invites local, state, national, and specialty bicycle organizations to post information online.

Marketplace

After getting into AOL's Marketplace, you can check the Classifieds Online (the Sporting & Athletic Goods folder in the General Merchandise Boards) for deals on bicycles and components. You can also browse around other online catalogues and companies to see who here is offering cycling-related merchandise.

Newsstand

The Newsstand on AOL gives you access to part or all of the articles available in scores of popular publications, including Bicycling Magazine Online. (Don't be fooled by Cycle World, which targets motorcyclists.) Other periodicals that you might want to peruse include Backpacker Magazine, the Chicago Tribune, MacWorld, PC World, the San Jose Mercury News, the New York Times, Time, and Wired. Syndicated columns and features are highlighted separately.

Reference Desk

America Online's Reference Desk is full of useful research material, all of which is easily searched by keyword. While several areas may have pieces of information about cycling, you'll find the Bulletin Board Services folder especially convenient for finding local and/or cycling-related BBSs. You can search by subject, state, or area code to find a system that meets your needs and interests.

Sports

Not surprisingly, you'll also find cycling news and information in the More Sports section of Sports News (or Choose a Sport) in AOL's Sports area. You'll need to scroll through the list to find Cycling, which provides regularly updated (several times a day during major events) racing news from the wire services. Coverage spans the globe and includes even minor road and track races.

Travel

If you're looking for adventure or just a relaxing tour on your bicycle, be sure to check out Outdoor Adventure Online in AOL's Travel area. Information about bicycle tours all over the world, from Baja to Tuscany is provided, as are details about state and national parks throughout North America. Bicycle guides and touring companies are reviewed, and contact information is provided. You'll find money-saving tips, country profiles, passport and Visa requirements for specific countries, timely health information (including

U.S. State Department travel warnings and advisories), and much more to help you plan your trip. The Weekend Sports Magazine includes fitness features and calendars of activities, adventures, and special events for the Pacific Northwest. Be sure to drop by the Message Center to "talk" with fellow adventure cyclists about specific companies, routes, countries, components, and other aspects of traveling on two wheels. Of course, the Travel area contains many useful resources whether you're traveling for leisure or business, with or without your bike.

Internet Connection

America Online's Internet Connection offers a bike-friendly on-ramp to the Internet. You can use e-mail, mailing lists, Usenet newsgroups, gopher servers, file transfer protocol, and World Wide Web. Even better, you can read Zen and the Art of the Internet online, a classic introduction to the Internet by Brendan Kehoe. You can also seek help from the Electronic Frontier Foundation, Wired, and the PC and Mac Communication Forums. The Internet Message Board helps steer you to hot sites on the Internet and lets you ask questions (and get answers in nontechnical language). In the Member Services area, you can ask AOL technical support questions about using the Internet and receive immediate answers. You'll read in the next chapter how each of the Internet tools works and can be used to locate the cycling resources available online.

America Online offers a simple interface to full Internet access.

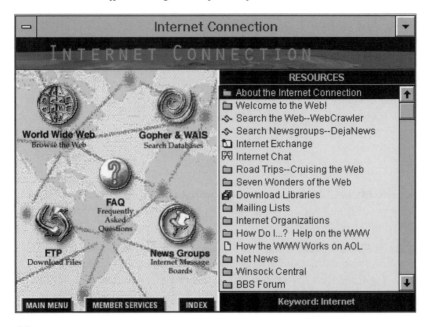

Chapter 3

Introduction to the Internet

You shouldn't be afraid of getting on the Internet. Those encyclopedic volumes about using the information superhighway aren't necessary to get your feet wet. You don't need to know the history of the Internet to use it. You won't need any arcane Unix commands to navigate cyberspace. You just need to sign on and look around for yourself.

The easiest and probably best way for a novice Internet user to see what's available is to go through a commercial service. Once again, you can take advantage of their free trial-period offers to determine whether you should stick with a commercial interface or get a dial-up Internet account, which is usually much less expensive if you plan to spend a lot of time online.

None of the commercial services provides Internet access in the same manner. GEnie and Delphi use predominantly text-based tools, which are fast and more comfortable for people accustomed to using keyboard commands and local BBSs (Delphi may have switched to a completely graphical interface by now). America Online, CompuServe, eWorld, and Prodigy use graphical interfaces that involve clicking on icons and moving the text cursor around with a mouse or trackball. Because AOL is particularly friendly to cyclists (Chapter 2), we'll comment on their Internet interface throughout this chapter. Most graphical interfaces are similar.

On the other hand, if your computer is your hobby, you might even enjoy installing several individual pieces of shareware to access and use the Internet (available—where else?—on BBSs, commercial services, and the Internet itself). In that case, add a general reference about the Internet to your library. Pick one published within the past year, the more recent the better, appropriate for your type of computer and level of expertise. (Alpha Books, IDG Books, Hayden Books, Que, and O'Reilly & Associates publish some of the best Internet reference books.)

You'll also find many nicely packaged (but more expensive) programs, such as Internet in a Box. Most Internet providers include a relatively user-friendly software suite with each account; ask about software when you call for pricing information. The individual names of these programs vary depending on the type of computer used, though some are available for multiple operating systems, such as Eudora (for e-mail), Netscape Navigator (for the World Wide Web), and TurboGopher (for gopherspace).

Electronic Mail

Electronic mail (e-mail) is the most common online tool. You can use an electronic mailbox (such as MCI Mail), a BBS account, a commercial online service (such as America Online or Delphi), a network terminal (at your company or university), or an Internet service provider (such as Netcom or Pipeline) to maintain an online connection. With e-mail, you can subscribe to mailing lists, write to cycling organizations, and communicate with cyclists around the globe. You can also use other Internet features, including file transfer protocol, World Wide Web, and gopher.

As with a letter to be mailed through the postal service, you'll need to know the electronic address of the person to whom you are writing. Appendix E includes e-mail addresses for bicycle-related companies, Appendix A lists some of the major cycling organizations, and addresses are provided for online sites and cyclists throughout the book. Writing an e-mail letter is just like writing any other letter except you will also need to give the message a "subject"—a few words describing the content or point of your note.

On America Online (shown below) and other accounts with a graphical interface, you'll find that e-mail is quite easy to use. You can create your own address book, compose your e-mail offline at your leisure, schedule your e-mail business (i.e., send and receive mail automatically) for times when the phone rates are less expensive, attach a file (useful for distributing routine information, such as a ride schedule or trail map), request a return receipt (so you know when the recipient read your note), and use many other helpful features.

Sending e-mail is not much different than sending a regular letter or memo: you need the recipient's address, a topic, and a message, which you can type in or copy from your word processing software.

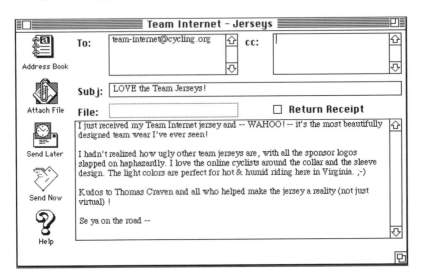

Mailing Lists

If you like receiving mail, you can be assured of signing on to a full e-mail box by subscribing to a mailing list or two. Mailing lists reach local, state, national, or international audiences with similar interests—whether a town riding club or a worldwide advocacy organization. Some lists exist mainly to make announcements, while others allow members to exchange advice, opinions, and experiences. If you subscribe to one list, wait at least a week before adding another subscription. You may find yourself overwhelmed by the number of messages that flood your e-mail box.

Many list owners use computer programs, such as Majordomo or Listserv, to handle routine tasks and answer basic questions. When you subscribe to these lists, you'll automatically receive information on how to participate with other members on the list and how to request specific documents (such as the list FAQ or frequently asked questions file). Please note the major commands below, which you type in the message body, not the subject line. When subscribing to mailing lists maintained by Listserv or Listproc, you'll need to add your full name (first and last) after the subscribe command. If your e-mail program automatically inserts a signature, include the word End after the last command. Otherwise, don't type your e-mail address or anything else in the message body.

Command	Purpose	Example
Subscribe Listname	Join list	`subscribe mtb`
Subscribe Listname-digest	Join digest form of list	`subscribe coaching-digest`
Unsubscribe Listname	Leave list	`unsubscribe ultra`
Info Listname	Get information about list	`info road-canada`
Who Listname	See who else is on list	`who team-internet`

You'll find that most cycling mailing lists are available on VeloNet (Chapter 4); Appendix D gives the name, focus, and subscription address of many bicycle-related mailing lists maintained there and elsewhere online. To learn more about using the Majordomo software at VeloNet, send an e-mail message to majordomo@cycling.org with the following two lines in the body (leave the subject line blank):

```
help
end
```

Unless you check your e-mail several times a day, you might prefer to subscribe to the digest version of the list. Normally, whenever anyone sends a message to the mailing list, the automated software immediately forwards this contribution to everyone who subscribes. On busy lists, this could mean dozens of individual e-mail notes piling up in your box in the course of a few hours. If you request the digest version, you'll get one big message that contains all the individual postings (usually with a table of contents at the top) for the last 24 hours.

When joining a mailing list that doesn't use automated software, you'll send a brief e-mail note addressed to the person who owns and operates the list, politely asking to subscribe. An address that includes -request@ often indicates that the mailing list is managed by a person rather than a computer program. You should always read the description of a mailing list's goals and topics when joining, and this is especially important when subscribing to an owner-maintained list. As you can imagine, it's a bit of work to keep adding and removing names from the subscription list.

America Online has a searchable database of mailing lists (go to the Internet Connection); some of the other commercial services keep a partial list of e-mail discussion groups. On AOL, each database entry explains how to join and leave the list, describes the list's goals and guidelines, and suggests keywords to identify similar lists. You'll also learn whether the mailing list can be read as a Usenet newsgroup, which may be more convenient than receiving the discussion messages via e-mail. On the other hand, you can identify all the members of a mailing list, whereas newsgroup audiences vary from minute to minute.

You'll find many cycling-related mailing lists maintained on VeloNet (see Appendix D for listings). America Online may help you find some additional lists that match your particular interests.

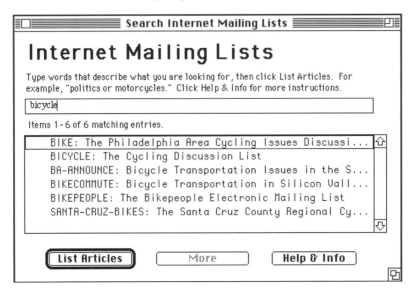

Usenet Newsgroups

Usenet newsgroups are like bike shop bulletin boards only much more active, more focused, and more widely read. Newsgroups are similar to mailing lists but are not centrally organized and do not maintain a subscriber list. Some newsgroups share messages with mailing lists on the same topic. Some share messages with BBS networks. Some use moderators, volunteers who review contributions and edit or censor messages that are inflammatory or based on rumor instead of fact (these newsgroups usually have the suffix -mod or -moderated as part of the name).

More than a dozen newsgroups address a wide range of cycling topics and regional cycling issues. However, whether you have access to every bicycle newsgroup depends on your network administrator, who decides which newsgroups to make available on the service or network. If you don't have access to a certain group that you'd like to join, try to contact the appropriate person about adding a specific newsgroup. Appendix C lists most of the widely available newsgroups and a few regional groups (many universities and cities have their own local newsgroup network).

Newsgroup messages include announcements, comments, or questions from subscribers all over the world. Sometimes questions are answered publicly on the newsgroup; sometimes they are answered via e-mail sent directly to the person who asked the question. New online cycling resources are announced on newsgroups. You'll also see "threads" in which one person

Most newsgroup readers allow you to scan through the subject lines of posted messages—some also let you search by subject word or author name.

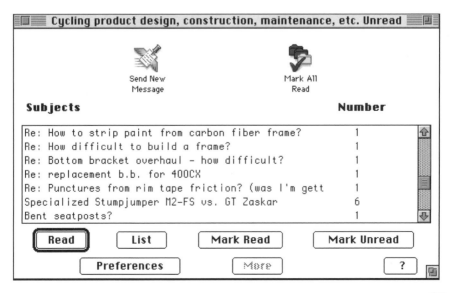

launches a discussion and everyone else joins in. Threads can address everything from preferences for bike components to disputes over a professional race finish to informal surveys of specific rides or trails. Be prepared for an incredible range of unshakable opinions and beliefs (read Chapter 14 for tips on joining online conversations).

Reading and contributing to newsgroups is easy and straightforward. On America Online, for example, you can locate and join newsgroups by searching through categories, by searching with a keyword, or by using the Expert Add feature (if you know the full name). Once subscribed to a group, you "read" it by scrolling through a list of individual messages and threads of several messages grouped under one subject line. Some newsgroup readers list messages in the order in which they are received; others alphabetize the subject lines, and still others force you to read each individual message in sequence (this archaic method is limited mainly to Unix-based readers).

You can easily post your own new message, add to an existing thread, or reply directly to the author via e-mail. Some newsgroup readers, such as the one used on AOL, make keeping track of which messages you do and don't want to read quite simple.

Many newsgroups, including rec.bicycles and rec.sport.triathlon, maintain composite files of frequently asked questions called FAQs (as in, "just the facts, ma'am"). These documents are invaluable additions to any cycling library. Always check for and read the newsgroup FAQ before asking your own question—it may have already been answered. You'll find the rec.bicycles FAQ and other useful newsgroup files conveniently collected in a gopher server described in Chapter 4.

Gopher

Gopher servers are the Internet's filing cabinets. They contain files, searchable databases, and links to other gopher directories. In other words, you may originally go to a gopher server located on a computer in San Francisco, open a folder that appears to be available on that computer (in California), and—without your knowing it—wind up reading documents that are actually stored on a computer in London. While this feature makes the Internet a powerful conveyer of information, it can also cause some frustrations. Making connections to computers all over the world takes time, and, as you probably aren't surprised to learn, not every computer on the Internet is always working in top form (more on dealing with the occasional Internet frustrations in Chapter 14).

Unless you have the exact address for a gopher resource (that's what this book is for), you'll probably want to use either the table of contents or the index to gopherspace. You can search the names and directory titles of gophers around the world with a program called Veronica (it probably won't be called that online though—you'll see something like Search All Gophers in the World). A local search tool, Jughead, usually shows up on your computer screen as Search This Gopher. Wide Area Information Servers (WAIS) (pronounced "wayz") index thousands of online documents around the world. As usual, how you view and use these special tools will vary with the manner in which you access the Internet. If you can use the World Wide Web, you'll probably prefer Internet search engines (Chapter 12) to gopher-related tools.

America Online simplifies using gophers and searching gopherspace. In the Internet Connection, rather than typing in gopher addresses, you go through folders of gopher servers organized by topic. The graphical interface helps you identify folders, text files, WAIS databases, telnet connections, images (though you can't view images with any gopher software, which is text-based, you can download them), and so on. Clicking on an open book icon will launch a WAIS search. You can also use AOL's version of Veronica (Search All Gophers) to find, go to, and view gopher servers and documents throughout gopherspace. Finally, you can go straight to a specific gopher not already listed by using AOL's Web Browser, which allows you to type in the gopher's address.

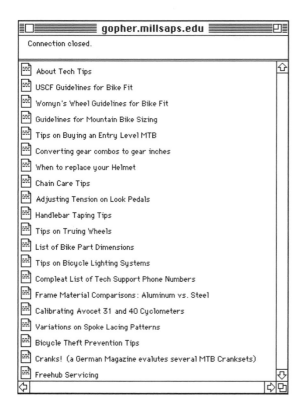

Steve King's Tech Tips gopher contains useful text documents that are stored at his site. Many gopher servers include folders, files, and WAIS searches, among other options.

World Wide Web

If you really want to have fun using the Internet, you will want to surf the World Wide Web (WWW). Most gopher servers can now be reached from a Web page, or the documents have been transferred from the gopher server to a Web site. The WWW is a multimedia network on the Internet, making full use of sounds, graphics, video, and interactive software. You move around the Web stream-of-consciousness style using programs known as "browsers." You'll find yourself browsing (also known as "surfing") around quite often. For example, you might start looking through a mountain bike Web site in Oregon for trail maps, decide just for kicks that you want to check out the off-road action in the United Kingdom, and find yourself reading about riding the Ho Chi Minh Trail—not at all what you set out to do.

Web sites offer graphics, text, e-mail forms, video, audio, and much more.
The Team Internet home page keeps members abreast of club news.

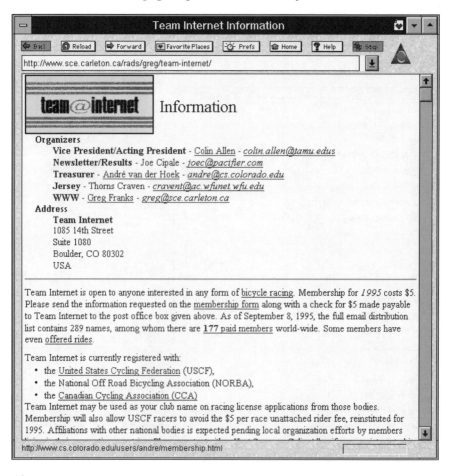

In gopherspace, links will mainly take you to other gopher servers. On the Web, links may open a text file, show you a graphic, start a video, launch a program (such as a spoke length calculator), sign a guest book, order a product, subscribe to a mailing list, or send an e-mail message.

You'll easily recognize these special Web links, which are known as "hypertext" links (since the text is active). Some are typed in a different format: underlined, bold, a different color, flashing on the screen, and so on. Many links are shown as icons or pictures that you click on. If you can't or choose not to view graphics (the pictures do slow things down), you'll see the underlined words or empty boxes where the image would normally load. With a strictly text browser such as Lynx, you'll see these links as sequential numbers or the word LINK in brackets.

If you know where you want to go, it's faster to get around by using a specific address or universal resource locator (URL). The URL starts with http:// or gopher:// or ftp://. You can also easily search the Web for specific topics, as explained in Chapter 12.

America Online has integrated its multipurpose browser with the rest of the service. You can launch the software from anywhere within AOL (i.e., you don't need to go to the Internet Connection), and usually links to appropriate Web sites are included within AOL forums. You'll find the Web browser fast and fun, though it may not work as well with every WWW link as more established browsers do (such as Netscape or Mosaic). As with most graphical browsers, you can keep a "hot list" of bookmarks to favorite Web sites, maintain a trail of where you've been surfing, and use the full range of multimedia features.

File Transfer Protocol

File transfer protocol (FTP) allows you to download files from computers all over the world to your own desktop. For example, you'll find an anonymous FTP site at Stanford University with USCF license application forms, race entry forms, rule books, and other documents. (The "anonymous" means that you don't need to have a user ID or know a password to gain access to the remote computer's hard drive.)

How easy it is to download these files will depend on the software you use: you may just point and click (graphical interface or as part of a Web browser), or you may need to know some special commands (shareware and Unix programs). If you're concerned about the amount of time you spend online, use FTP in the evening or on weekends, when these sites are less busy.

If you need to locate a particular file, ask Archie. Archie is a program that searches files using a keyword (on AOL and other graphical interfaces), file name, directory name, or group of characters that you supply. Be very specific, or you may find your request for spoke length calculators (using just the keyword "spoke") turning up thousands of unrelated matches, such as those containing the word "spoken." You can get help using Archie by sending an e-mail message with the word `Help` in the subject line (blank message body) to archie@archie.sura.net or archie@archie.unl.edu (among many others).

Remember, as you learned in Chapter 1, a computer virus can infect executable files (software) and macros, so you should use antivirus software to check any programs that you download. Plain text and graphic files cannot be infected. Many Internet volunteer operators examine submitted files for viruses, but you can't always count on this.

As with its other Internet tools, America Online's anonymous FTP area (and corresponding tool integrated in the Web browser) is simple and straightforward. You can select from among AOL's Favorite Sites or type in an address. To transfer a file to your hard drive, select the file you want and click the Download Now icon. You can monitor the transfer's progress and amount of time required through a bar graph, and you can also ask that the transfer be temporarily suspended until later in your AOL session. America Online does the entire Internet a great service by including mirror sites of the major FTP areas; that is, AOL duplicates all the files available at, for example, MIT's FTP site (rtfm.mit.edu), which, by the way, is where you'll find copies of FAQs for most Usenet newsgroups.

File transfer protocol lets you select files to copy onto your computer.

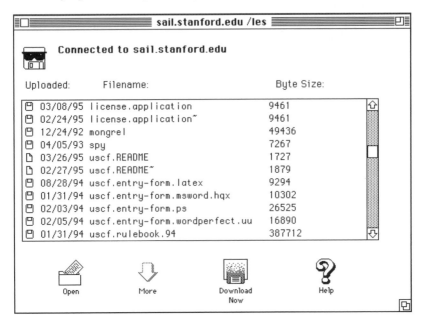

Telnet

While the other Internet tools help you navigate through cyberspace, telnet actually allows you to use a remote computer as though it were on your desk. Sometimes you'll need a user ID and password to gain access, but public telnet sites provide this information automatically. Telnet is mainly used for searching large, centrally located databases or exploring freenets and BBSs. For example, if you were looking for published books and articles on a cycling topic, you could telnet to the Uncover database at CARL Corporation (database.carl.org) and search by subject. None of the cycling resources discussed in this book requires the use of telnet.

Internet Relay Chat

You learned about the Bike Chat Room on America Online in Chapter 2. Internet relay chat (IRC) allows international conferences in publicly available rooms (known as "channels"). Channel names should identify the users or purpose, and the channels themselves are usually available 24 hours a day. Because literally thousands of people can join an IRC channel, you will probably find it slower than a chat session on a commercial service or BBS.

Only one bike-related IRC channel had been announced when we last checked: #mtnbike (topic: Mountain Bikers of the World Unite). According to one active member, Tumult in Canada, "The best time to find people is on the weekends. Talk usually consists of answering questions, offering opinions on various bikes, parts and accessories, or talk about good places to ride or rides that we've been on."

You'll need special software (as always) to participate in an IRC meeting. Delphi offers IRC access (as do many Internet providers), but none of the other commercial services did at last check.

First, you need to log onto an IRC server (such as irc-2.mit.edu or cs-pub.bu.edu); then you'll /join a channel (such as #mtnbike). You can see what channels are available by using the /list command, but you'll probably want to try to join a specific channel first—listing all channels can take a few minutes and may produce a seemingly endless list of choices. You should be able to /join #mtnbike anytime.

If you use IRC, you should give yourself a nickname (/nick) *before* joining a channel. Other people on the channel will then "see" you as your nickname. You can get help anytime (/help) and can see who else is in a specific channel if you're looking to meet someone (for example, /who #mtnbike). Leaving the channel (/exit) is just as easy. You'll find additional help for using IRC on the WWW (http://urth.acsu.buffalo.edu/irc/WWW/ircdocs.html) and through your Internet provider.

Even this isn't the end of the line in terms of Internet tools. You'll see references to Talk, Finger, Whois, Netfind, Knowbots, and many more Internet utilities not discussed here. In addition, new technologies are coming online at an incredible pace. We've only covered the resources directly relevant to participating in the online cycling community. As we said earlier, if you're interested in exploring everything, you should read through the most recent general Internet reference books to learn more about all the nooks and crannies of cyberspace and all the shortcuts for getting there.

Web pages can link up with most of the Internet: gopher servers, FTP directories, mailing lists, e-mail addresses, Usenet newsgroups, and more. Brent Soderberg's Virtual Breakaway also includes a link that will drop you off at a random cycling-related Web site.

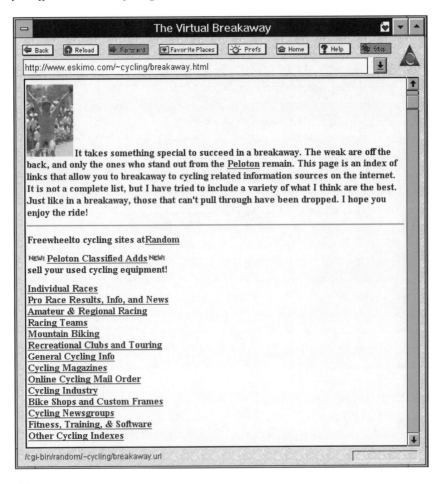

Chapter 4

General Cycling

Of the hundreds, perhaps thousands, of places online that offer cycling information, only a small portion are completely dedicated to one topic. The sites described in this chapter could be of use to just about any cyclist because they include information and links for a broad range of cycling interests. Several would be good additions to your Web browser hot list. Be sure also to check the sites reviewed in Chapter 12, which provide outstanding catalogs of online cycling resources. In this chapter, special attention is devoted first to the premier online cycling resource: VeloNet.

VeloNet—the Global Cycling Network
http://cycling.org/

As described by its organizer/owner/operator Patrick Goebel, "VeloNet™ is an electronic information desk for cyclists." VeloNet offers one-stop shopping for all the bicycle-related information and advice you could possibly need. Although the bulk of information provided here is now accessed through the World Wide Web, you'll find that most bicycle-related mailing lists are maintained at cycling.org with Majordomo software. Messages submitted to these lists are archived and can be read on the Web pages. Nonprofit groups can take advantage of VeloNet's FreeWeb as well. Be sure to thank Patrick and others for their voluntary efforts when you stop by.

All online bike paths lead to VeloNet.

VeloNet can be easily read with both graphical and text browsers. The network is growing rapidly, and frequent visitors will appreciate the "What's New?" directory, which chronologically lists additions and organizational changes to the site. Perhaps the best resources are the VeloNet Phone Books, which explain how to contact bicycle organizations around the world, and the VeloWeb, where you'll find links to cycling sites and documents.

Mailing Lists

If you can access the Internet only through e-mail, you're in luck. VeloNet has more than one hundred mailing lists from which to choose (see Appendix D). Electronic mailing lists are discussed in Chapter 3, where you'll find the commands for subscribing, unsubscribing, and managing your lists.

VeloWeb

VeloNet's VeloWeb is a cycling library in which the books are shelved all over the world. Each section lists Internet resources—Web pages, gopher servers, individual documents—and mailing lists related to the main topic. Large areas, such as racing, are broken into several subtopics. The mailing lists have brief descriptions, and the Web sites have clear, descriptive names. Nonprofit organizations and clubs will find VeloNet's FreeWeb service here.

The VeloWeb

- Advocacy
- BMX
- Calendars
- Commercial
- Commuting
- Miscellaneous Pages
- Mountain Biking
- Multi-Topic Pages
- Personal Cycling Pages
- Racing
- Regional Pages
- Safety
- Tandem Riding
- Touring and Vacations
- Training, Health & Fitness
- Traveling with your Bicycle
- Triathlons, Duathlons & other Multisport Events
- TV Network Coverage and Schedules
- Unicycling
- Usenet Newsgroups
- Vehicle Code
- The VeloNet FreeWeb

The VeloWeb (formerly the Reading Room) gives you access to ride suggestions and calendars, bicycle industry news, race results, travel tips, and a wealth of cycling information.

Phone Books

If you need to contact just about any bicycle organization anywhere in the world, you need to go to VeloNet. You can do a keyword search to locate clubs and other groups that represent your region or interest, or you can work your way through regional subdirectories for each main category: International, Africa, Australia, Canada, Europe, New Zealand, United Kingdom, and United States. Each entry will list online and offline means of contacting the organization, what the group has to offer (newsletter, meetings, projects, etc.), and other notes. You can usually send a message to the contact person, subscribe to the group's mailing list (e-mail forms are provided on the page), and go to the associated Web page if one is available.

CLAIRE

If you'd like to monitor the benefits of your bike commuting, you'll want to join CLAIRE, the Campaign for Clean Air and Exercise. You sign up to "play" CLAIRE by submitting a form available on VeloNet. You'll be given a lifetime ID number that will be used to record all car trips and mileage saved by cycling, walking, carpooling, and other environmentally friendly means (you submit your data monthly). CLAIRE collects statistics from all over the world and generates reports of emissions and fuel saved through alternative transportation, organized by individual, country, city, state, or province.

Contributing to VeloNet

You can contribute to VeloNet by informing the network of a cycling-related Internet resource not currently listed (send its URL to newurl@cycling.org). If you're interested in transferring your mailing list or starting a list for your club, you can ask to be added (write to newlist@cycling.org). To list your organization in the VeloNet phone books, send an empty message to newphone@cycling.org and you'll receive a form to complete and submit.

Around the beginning of 1994, it occurred to me that bicycling advocates around the world could use a medium by which to communicate, coordinate and otherwise discuss issues related to cycling. Since I am both a cyclist and a computer network administrator in the heart of Silicon Valley, it seemed natural that I should set up such a service. The result is VeloNet, an information desk for cyclists on the Internet that combines a Web site (http://cycling.org/) with a mailing list server (majordomo@cycling.org).

Patrick Goebel

47

Bicycle@Yukon
gopher://info.cren.net/11/archives

The Bicycle e-mail discussion group is an incredible resource for any cyclist with an electronic address. You subscribe by sending the message `sub-scribe bicycle` *your name* (inserting your own name) to listproc@list.cren.net (formerly *@yukon*.cren.net); you participate by sending messages to bicycle@list.cren.net. If you can use the gopher address above (open the Bicycle folder), you can read the list's archives, which are organized by year and month and are also searchable by keyword. Either way, you'll find advice, encouragement, news, humor, results, announcements, and more. It's somewhat like receiving the rec.bicycles newsgroups via e-mail.

Bicycling Community Page
http://www.cs.wisc.edu/~condon/sd.html

Although it serves the Madison and Dane County area of Wisconsin, you'll find a lot of valuable help and information at the Bicycling Community Page. Scott Rose serves as the overall editor with plenty of help from other conributors (such as Pascal Balthrop, who created the graphical index shown below). Some of the sections are devoted entirely or almost entirely to local interests: Events, News & Info, Commuting, Off-Road, and Spare Parts. No matter where you live, you'll find useful information and links in the Weather, Bike Shops, Racing, Tourists, Advocacy, and Bike Groups sections. The Online Stuff page is one of the best organized indices to online cycling resources (mailing lists and Web pages are explained separately). It's worth a place on your hot list.

The Bicycling Community Page serves a much larger cycling community than that in Wisconsin.

Cascade Bicycle Club
http://cascade.org/cbc.html

The Cascade Bicycle Club, the largest club in the Unites States, has a nice set of searchable local and general cycling pages maintained by Kevin Fink. If you live in the Seattle area, you'll love all the detailed ride, event, club, legal, weather, commuting, advocacy, and transportation information. They also have a Bicycling Visitor's Guide to Seattle and a section on riding with children in the Puget Sound area. Any cyclist would be interested in reading the Bicycling Information section, which includes the rec.bicycles FAQ plus dozens of individual topics broken out from (and supplementing) the FAQ: General Information, Equipment Reviews and Information, Do It Yourself Info, Advice, Training, Medical Information, and Software. The page of links, maintained by Mark Allyn, is terrific and includes comments on what to expect from each site.

Cyber Cyclery
http://www.cyclery.com/

Cyber Cyclery is a well-organized commercial site that should be of interest to most cyclists. Cyber Cyclery covers cycling equipment manufacturers, tour operations from all over the world, and news from racing and industry, including Interbike coverage. Mountain bikers will want to check the Ultimate Mountain Bike Calendar ("vision and work of Don Smyrl"), which includes riding and camping trips, a suggested maintenance schedule, and a birthday list for professional racers (a few roadies slip in, such as Eddy Merckx and Greg Lemond, both born in June). Print magazines with online samples and information include Cycling Science, Bike Culture Quarterly (BCQ) and the BCQ Encyclopedia, and Dirt Rag; separately you'll find a long list of cycling magazines with online and offline addresses. The Reading directory is one amalgamated online magazine with articles, interviews, and product reviews taken from several sources. Links to races and other cycling events are included in the Racing section. Bicycling Organizations and Associations are also conveniently listed here. Finally, you'll find a comprehensive, well-organized list of links to other cycling sites guaranteed to keep you busy for days.

Cybercyclists should all plan to stop at Cyber Cyclery.

Cycle Expo
http://www.cycle-expo.com/cycle-expo/

Peter Grabowsky has launched a central commercial cycling site that offers the usual benefits of comprehensive links, industry news and contacts, and well-organized cycling information (Cycling Products, Cycling Services, WWW Cycling Resources). Cycle Expo is updated biweekly (sometimes more frequently) and includes (or will soon) local documents, Usenet newsgroups, a bulletin board for buying/selling/swapping bicycle-related items, a monthly newsletter, another bulletin board for cycling banter, and several interactive e-mail forms. You'll find this a good place to stop when you need to find an obscure manufacturer or a regional cycling resource.

Cycling
http://www.voicenet.com/leisure/sports/cycling/

George Theall has long maintained a terrific collection of resources useful to anyone on two wheels. Links and documents are organized in clearly titled categories: commuting by bike; electronic forums; laws affecting cyclists; racing; shopping; and other sources of cycling info on the Net. New items are flagged as such, and everything gets a sentence or two explaining what you'll find or read. His list of links includes most of the top cycling sites on the Net. In addition, he separately keeps a page devoted to the Philadelphia area and the Mid-Atlantic region (his racing calendar is superb).

Great Outdoors Recreation Pages (GORP)
http://WWW.gorp.com/gorp/activity/biking.htm

The Great Outdoors Recreation Pages, owned and maintained by Diane Greer and Greer Consulting Services, are just that: a comprehensive Web site for outdoor activities ranging from bird watching to windsurfing almost anywhere in the world. GORP's cycling resources are excellent. You can find basic information on a wide range of topics, such as biking in national parks, and descriptions of cycling sites throughout the Internet. These links include other index pages (see Chapter 12), regional sites, information sources, and biking clubs and organizations. A handy index to the biking pages and back to the main GORP pages (with their tremendous travel assistance and outdoor adventure tips) make research here easy and enjoyable.

The Great Outdoors Recreation Pages are truly great for cyclists.

Heiner's Home Page
http://www-2.informatik.umu.se/hs

Heiner Schorn has an international list of links that separates those sites in German and Dutch from those in English. All manner of cycling resources are included, many among the best on the Internet. Information valuable to commuters, tourists, road racers, mountain bikers, and bike advocates can be found here. He also keeps track of a few human-powered vehicle sites. If you glance at his home page, you'll find several other categories of sites, such as German, Environment, Music, Weather, Funny, Computer, and Newspapers and Journals.

Jørn's Cycling Homepage
http://www.fysel.unit.no/dahls/cycling.html
ftp ftp.unit.no/local/biking/velo20.zip
ftp draco.acs.uci.edu/pub/rec.bicycles/velo20.zip

Jørn Dahl-Stamnes has a cycling home page of interest to the local (Norwegian) and global cycling community. Jørn is known throughout the Internet as the author of Velocipede, a comprehensive cycling training log program that can also keep track of wheel and tire usage, maintain a running account of cycling-related expenses, calculate gearing and spoke length, and much more. Jørn maintains a mailing list to announce new releases, answer questions, report bugs, and receive upgrade suggestions. Elsewhere on his Web page, you can learn about the world's first bike lift (sort of like a ski lift—it helps cyclists get up hills), located in Trondheim, Norway. He also has uncompressed (text) and compressed (.zip) files of the rec.bicycles FAQ and an article about riding in a paceline. Be sure to read his tour reports; you'll enjoy his accounts and probably pick up some training and racing tips. His hot list covers road and mountain biking, commercial sites, race coverage, training and technique, and central catalogs of other cycling resources.

> *Cycling is a great sport. You can cycle for hours for mile after mile, enjoying mother nature. Still, you cannot stay on your bike forever. Resting is a necessary part of your training. But this does not mean you have to stop cycling. With a computer you can get on a virtual bicycle and take a ride in Cyberspace, where you can ride for hours without getting exhausted … imagine yourself participating in other cyclists' great adventures.*
> Jørn Dahl-Stamnes

(Pittsburgh) Bicycling Home Page
http://www.cs.cmu.edu/~jdg/bike/

John Greiner keeps up a regional page that serves the global cycling community well. Of course, much of the information is particularly useful to people living in western Pennsylvania, but John keeps the entire site current. The page is organized according to what you as a cyclist need or want to do: Preparing you and your equipment to bike; Where to bike; Health, safety, and skills; Racing; Information local to … [not just Pittsburgh]; Bicycling-related magazines and e-zines; and Other cycling information. Some of the practical tips are taken from newsgroup messages on a common theme (such as truing wheels), while others are links to information-packed sites, such as Steve King's Tech Tips gopher server (Chapter 8).

rec.bicycles FAQ
http://draco.acs.uci.edu/rbfaq/
http://www.cis.ohio-state.edu/hypertext/faq/usenet/bicycles-faq/top.html
gopher draco.acs.uci.edu
ftp draco.acs.uci.edu/pub/rec.bicycles/

Mike Iglesias manages the rec.bicycles FAQ, which is posted around the 15th of every month to rec.bicycles.misc (announcements about the FAQ are posted to all the rec.bicycles newsgroups). The FAQ is also available in a gopher server, via FTP (which includes many other useful files, such as software, pictures, and text documents), and in hypertext format on the Web. Archives of other useful messages from rec.bicycles as well as training software and bicycle-related graphics are also available. Dozens, perhaps hundreds, of people have contributed to this amazing compilation of bicycle knowledge, and you won't want to miss it. Make it one of your first stops.

I had been reading rec.bicycles for about a year or so when the need for a FAQ arose. I constructed one from postings I had saved, and it has mushroomed from there. After about 3 years, it has grown to five parts, and there's an anonymous FTP area, a gopher server, and now a Web server. I get a few contributions every month from readers; most go into the FAQ unless they are too big, and those go into the FTP area. Currently I'm getting about 10,000 hits a month on the gopher server, 2,000 on the Web server, and about 3,000 file transfers out of the FTP area, so you can see that these areas are useful to cyclists around the world.
Mike Iglesias

Trento Bike Pages
http://www-math.science.unitn.it/Bike/

Andreas Caranti's Trento Bike Pages should be your first online stop in Europe. Information is available mainly in English but also in Italian, French, and German. You'll be able to plan for a cycling trip (on- or off-road) in almost any country, read accounts of tours and trips by others, and check announcements for scheduled rides, competitions, and festivals. This site is a delight even if you never make it to Albania or one of the many other countries included. Andreas also has information about Eurobike, the mailing list for European cyclists (member bios and photos included), and the Eurobike Racing Team (long comment in Italian). You'll also find an annotated list of links to other cycling sites with a special emphasis on European pages but plenty of Web stops around the globe. Among the European links are Europole and the European Cyclists' Federation pages.

U.S. Bicycling Hall of Fame
http://www.nj.com/bike/hof/top.hof.html

The U.S. Bicycling Hall of Fame, available on NJ Online Biking (part of New Jersey Online, managed by Susan Mernit), is designed to "honor the sport of cycling, chronicle the history of cycling in America, and provide a center for information and education of the sport and pastime." Competitive and recreational cyclists alike are celebrated here for a wide range of contributions to the sport of cycling. You can read the biographical sketches and sometimes view pictures of inductees, read a history of the Hall of Fame, go through the Hall's exhibits, and learn more about how inductees are nominated and selected.

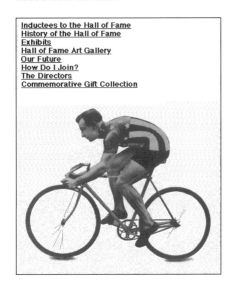

If you can't make it to Somerville, New Jersey, to visit the U.S. Bicycling Hall of Fame in person, be sure to stop at the well-designed Web site dedicated to honoring the heros of our sport.

VeloLinQ

http://www.wsmith.com/veloling/mainmenu.html

"Updated daily, VeloLinQ is your Internet source for current and mountain bicycling news, the hottest products, online cycling magazines, and much more!" This about sums up the value of VeloLinQ, which is continuing to evolve into a dynamic e-zine and commercial hub for anything on two wheels. The main directory, accessible with graphical or text interfaces, takes you to late-breaking news (including Interbike coverage), useful information, and links related to all the major aspects of cycling. Databases are searchable, individual pages are well organized and easy to browse, and the news is fresh. You'll appreciate its consistency, timeliness, and wealth of resources. Special features include free Web pages and entries for race promoters and clubs and other nonprofit cycling groups (VeloLinQ plans to sponsor teams and races). VeloLinQ also plans an Ultimate Bike Giveaway (a good one for anyone obsessed with their body/bike weight) and nearly real-time coverage of the Olympic cycling events. Dan Swofford and WebSmith promise all this and much more, so you'll probably want a bookmark for VeloLinQ on your hot list.

VeloLinQ, already a hot spot in cycling cyberspace, promises even more.

NEWS	Cycling News - Links to insider info, new product releases, and racing news
CLUBS	Clubs, racing news, team news, and racing results
MAGAZINES	Magazines - Links to bicycling magazines
SHOWCASE	Product Showcase - Veloling manufacturer's and retailer's showcase, recall information
DIRECTORY	Manufacturer Directory - Our searchable database
LINQS	Cool linqs to other cycling sites... but please make it back home safely!
TOURING	Touring and Commuting - Info on biking around the world or just to the office
FITNESS	Fitness and Training - The latest info on fitness and training
VeloLinQ	VeloLinQ - About VeloLinQ and how to contact us
WebSmith	WebSmith - About WebSmith, the creators of VeloLinQ

Chapter 5

Mountain Biking

Mountain bikers will find no shortage of dirt online. New and experienced mountain bikers will benefit from the many sources of advice on riding skills and bike maintenance, component and bike reviews, and shared war stories and photos, only a fraction of which are listed here. Regional (Chapter 13) and racing (Chapter 6) resources specific to mountain biking are also available. You'll find more off-road information on several of the sites reviewed in Chapter 4, and many magazines devoted to the sport are online (Chapter 9). Finally, don't miss #mtnbike (IRC channel), described in Chapter 3.

Arizona Mountain Biking Page
http://www.primenet.com/~bikeboy/az_mtb.html

Bill Jamison wants the world to know that Arizona is a "very cool place to ride." You'll find everything you need to know about mountain biking in this desert state: weather, bike rentals, brush fire alerts, trails, and race schedules. You can also read articles about mountain biking etiquette, precautions for desert riding (everything from prehydration to tangling with cacti), and crash experiences. Bill (aka Bikeboy) also has his training regimen online and plans to add a section on maintaining your mountain bike.

Beetle's Bike Page
http://www.Quake.Net/~baileyc/mtb.html

Chris "Beetle" Bailey introduces his page with the slogan "Ride fast, take chances." He should know, having managed the Pedros team, raced for Shaklee, and survived a potentially fatal crash. One of his best features is Beetle's Tire Notes, a thorough, well-written review of available tires on the market, with separate notes for front and rear tires. Be sure to check out the Fat Tire Fotos page (Chapter 6) and Chris' well-organized links.

> *The World Wide Web has created a new resource for cyclists. The best part is how quickly information becomes available. When Fabio Casartelli died in the Tour de France, information was available the same day. Through sites like Fat Tire Fotos, race results, articles, and photos are available within a day or two. In addition, the Web has honest and opinionated equipment reviews. Cyclists who pay for the products, use them daily, and aren't being paid to test or review them often provide candid, useful feedback.*
> Chris Bailey

Bike Bits Page
http://rdg.mat.liv.ac.uk/~steve/angela.html

Steve Wooding has a terrific home page of interest to mountain bikers (links and photos included), but his Bike Bits Page, Angela II, provides a great review of dozens of bicycle components. He writes about how he has used the component or accessory, gives a concise list of pros and cons, and shows several photos, which are particularly nice in showing how well various items hold up under wear. Not surprisingly, you'll also find Steve contributing to the rec.bicycles newsgroups.

Coghead Corner
http://www.teleport.com/~bazzle/coghead.shtml

Mark Whitney invites you to Coghead Corner, his own little mud puddle in cyberspace, where you'll find a solid collection of links and documents. For information local to Portland, Oregon, you can check out top trails, keep track of the weather, and learn where to rent a mountain bike. Mark has the IMBA Rules of the Trail and Trail Rating documents and a link to the Stolen Bike Registry. He also has links to a couple dozen great cycling sites, including companies, magazines, organizations, and user home pages.

Cool Places to Ride
ftp://ftp.cts.com/pub/alans/coolplcs.html
ftp ftp.cts.com/pub/alans/gallery

Ray Schumacher lets you see where you're going by providing photographs of dozens of off-road riding areas. He shows trails in California, Utah, Baja California (Mexico), and other locations organized by city or region. You can read a caption of the picture and check its size before taking the time to view or download anything. Ray also has a huge list of custom frame builders (contact information, frame material, and other specs) and links to some great off-road sites on the Web.

Ray Schumacher has dozens of photos of mountain biking trails, such as this shot of John's Canyon in Utah.

Dictionary of Off-Road Bike Slang

http://world.std.com/~jimf/biking/slang.html
http://www.public.iastate.edu/~midnite/slang.html [Jerry Dunn's]

Jim Frost maintains a dictionary (started by Tom Purvis and Jerry Dunn with contributions from a dedicated staff) you won't find in your local library reference section. The crew from rec.bicycles.off-road explains everything from "bacon" to "unobtanium." You'll learn why you don't want to have a yard sale, particularly in a vegetable tunnel. You can also read a little history about where this colorful collection of words originated.

Fat Tire Wire

http://www.fat-tire-wire.com/ftw/

Fat Tire Wire, formerly known as RaceWeb, has grown into a one-stop off-road site full of regional databases, weather and travel information, and advocacy groups. You can search separate databases for races (including MTB triathlons), rides, and riding resources, look through a photo gallery and mountain biking cartoons by William Nealy, or join the Fat Tire Forum. Be sure to visit the Mountain Bike Museum and Hall of Fame. You'll also find the usual links to mountain biking magazines and companies. RaceWeb itself also offers a comprehensive, well-organized collection of information about and links to mountain bike races, teams, and results. You'll be given the name, date, location, and type of race plus a phone number to call for additional information. You can jump straight to the Image Maps or use more conventional menus for International Racing, U.S. Racing, Racing Series, and Teams. Within each of these sections, you'll find regional subdirectories. Chris Johnson and Alpenglow Communications have big plans for Fat Tire Wire, so stay tuned.

Fat Tire Wire has become much more than a MTB racing center.

What's New: Fat Tire Wire and RaceWeb

Check out our plans to have a comprehensive listing of races and results!

- USA Calendar - updated race schedule for the United States.
- RaceSearch - a database search of races by date, region, and race type. For you DH'ers this means finding only the downhill races. Online race registration forms, race descriptions and prize listing. Free listing for promoters.
- Race Results - results for not only the Nationals. This was the most requested item in 1995. Free results posting for race promoters. Tell your local promoter to get it online.
- Tip of The Week - mountain bike racing and riding tips. Contributions welcome.
- Race Teams Directory - a full listing of all mountain bike racing teams, their sponsors, and the riders who really make it happen. Free listing of team rosters.
- MTB Triathalons - Yes, this is it, the ultimate in physical abuse. We are not responsible for people who enter this zone.

The Mountain Bike Pages
http://catless.ncl.ac.uk/mtb/README.html

Lindsay Marshall offers an extensive set of Mountain Bike Pages that may
have a U.K. flavor but would taste good to any mountain biker. You'll find
Kids Stuff (how to find and fit a MTB to a child), a Noticeboard, mainly
local routes, and a wide assortment of nicely organized links. Lindsay has
several magazines from which to choose (plus a humorous if cynical charac-
terization of all online MTB magazines), a collection of commercial sites,
mountain bike race schedules and results, and a regional grouping of Web
connections organized on a world map and accessible via text lists by country
or region. You'll learn about cycling newsgroups, mailing lists, e-mail addresses, and BBS conferences, too. You can also work your way to the
Vegetarian Pages (Chapter 10).

Mountain Bike Trials Riding
http://www.cs.nmt.edu/~andy/trials.html

Andy Mayer gives a quick summary of mountain bike trials (he's working on
a separate Usenet newsgroup, which may be available by now), including the
rules, the obstacles, and the equipment involved, as shown in several photos.

The Mountain Bike Pages cater to mountain bikers of all ages.

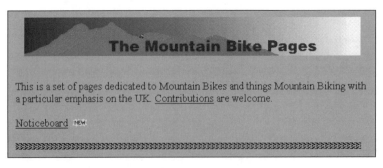

*Running a World Wide Web site for mountain bikers is a great thing to do.
You get lots of friendly e-mail, some with new information for your pages,
some just saying "Hello!" Often people send open invitations to go out
riding if you are in their neck of the woods. Best of all is when someone
visits where you live, and you get the chance to meet them in real life, ride
with them, and help them with advice on local routes and conditions. The
downside is that their bike is usually more trick than yours. ...*
Lindsay Marshall

Mountain Biking
http://xenon.stanford.edu/~rsf/mtn-bike.html

Ross Finlayson maintains one of the most complete mountain biking sites you'll find, organized in the following broad categories: Mountain biking in the San Francisco Bay area, Mountain biking in other areas—USA, Canada, British Columbia, New Brunswick, Ontario, Europe, France, the Netherlands, Sweden, Ukraine, the U.K., Vietnam, Nepal, Mount Everest, New Zealand—Race information, Advice, Pictures, and Miscellaneous. Each listing gets at least a few words to describe what you'll find … just enough to be helpful without lengthening the page unnecessarily. You'll find lots of nicely organized useful information rather than a laundry list of every possible MTB site online. Fun stuff includes mountain biking cartoons by Bill Watterson (Calvin & Hobbes); useful stuff includes health tips from Dr. Douglas Ehrenberg, Andy Mayer's mountain bike trials riding page, and a Maine bike mechanic's advice column (Chapter 8). At the top of the page (after Dave Le's title graphic, shown below), you'll be given the option to check This Month's Featured Area, which is usually featured for good reason.

MTB
http://www.etek.chalmers.se/~e4osbeck/mtb

Among the European mountain bikers who maintain Web sites, Christer Osbeck is holding down the fort in Sweden. He covers some local interests, including the Swedish race season (in Swedish), clubs around Göteborg, and the Nightmare Classic, in which "the race conditions are usually very muddy and dark." Crister has a well-rounded collection of links, including manufacturers and retailers, organizations and clubs, magazines and e-zines, mailing lists, e-mail addresses, and "personal home pages of real freaks." He also has a few photos and reports from the World Championships. Some of his links are unique, so stop here if you're tired of the same old stuff.

All off-road cybertrails point to Mountain Biking.

Featured in "Mountain Bike" magazine, May 1995, page 12!

MuDSLuTs
http://www.rubyslippers.com/funhouse/index2.html

In his attempt to "establish an internet electronic base camp" for online mountain bikers, Geff Hinds has created MuDSLuTs to serve the northwest region of the United States and everyone else beyond. The quarterly MuDSLuTs newsletter covers U.S. mountain biking news, industry news, links to weather sites, and a link to races and rides in the northwest. The Travel section reviews prime mountain biking destinations, providing travel tips, area bike shops, recommended rides, and suggested restaurants and other travel information. You can view multimedia ride accounts in the Virtual MuDSLuT; check out the Bull Board, with its KooLer (photo album), Finger (new rides and biking locations), Whine List, and links to Usenet newsgroups. MuDSLuTs' Techno Weenie gives no-nonsense reviews of products (photos included) near and dear to mountain bikers. The MuDSLuTs Yellow Pages comprise links to other cycling sites, commercial stops, and online mountain biking meccas (a running personal commentary on the best sites), while the clubs section will take you to regional mountain biking groups and organizations. Separately (under Etc, Etc) you'll find links to several other important sites, such as online magazines, general sports sites, and the Dictionary of Mountain Bike Slang.

New England Mountain Biking Association (NEMBA)
http://www.ultranet.com/~kvk/nemba.html

NEMBA is a not-for-profit organization dedicated to promoting land access for mountain bikers in New England, but cybercyclists will find useful material here no matter where they ride offline. Web editor Ken Koellner keeps the page up to date and includes practical information, such as A Mountain Bicyclist's Guide to Responsible Riding and IMBA Rules of the Trail, plus a selection of Cool Links. Local information includes a list of good deeds by New England mountain bikers, places to ride throughout the region (detailed directions and trail conditions), a list of books about mountain biking in New England, and details about NEMBA and its mission. The page is well integrated and makes good use of hypertext links.

Don't miss the "internet electronic base camp" for online mountain bikers.

New Zealand Mountain Bike Web
http://www.wcc.govt.nz/extern/kennett/homepage.htm

Paul Kennet maintains the New Zealand Mountain Bike Web, a one-stop, searchable site full of information about the sport and the nation. You'll find a calendar of events, many race results, mountain bike rides and guides for New Zealand, and a ticket to Planet Mountain Bike.

Rob's Mountainbike Page
http://www.xs4all.nl/~rcoende/index.html

Rob Coenders, a "Dutch mountainbiker on the information highway," keeps a dynamic site that you'll enjoy breezing through, especially if you're signing on from Europe. Rob gives you a taste of mountain biking in the Netherlands with the Dutch Mountainbike Calendar, Trails in the Netherlands, and other Dutch and international (mainly racing) links. You'll also find an organized list of his favorite Web pages (some, such as the Dutch Bicycle Path, are, not surprisingly, in Dutch) and several mountain biking photos.

Women's Mountain Biking and Tea Society (WOMBATS)
http://www.wombats.org/

Jacquie Phelan founded WOMBATS, which has chapters in California, Colorado, Connecticut, Maryland, Massachusetts, Michigan, New York, Oregon, Utah, and Washington, to encourage women of all ages and backgrounds to give mountain biking a try. You can learn more about Jacquie and the WOMBATS online. Hadley Taylor maintains the WOMBATS Web page (not to mention her own terrific home page), where you can peruse the WOMBAT art gallery (it's worth the trip), read the WOMBATS newsletter, and check out the WOMBAT Web links.

Women mountain bikers will find support online and on the trail.

Worldguide
http://www.worldguide.com

Worldguide Online offers "Virtual Maps of the Earth" plus a great online magazine with such sections as Health & Fitness, Nutrition, Mountain Biking, and High Impact. You'll most appreciate the three-dimensional terrain animations, maps, and elevation data for locations throughout the world. The Mountain Bike Atlas is a trail and travel guide and includes riding tips and tricks, a technology report, and trail descriptions and topographic maps. The American Wilderness Series, organized by region of the country, shows three-dimensional animations and two-dimensional maps based on LANDSAT data (such as Mammoth Cave, the Grand Teton Range, Bryce Canyon, Guadalupe, Yosemite, and Crater Lake). Elsewhere, you'll find tutorials on human anatomy, strength training, cardiovascular fitness, nutrition, and sports medicine, plus Highplanet, a separate magazine that emphasizes natural and alternative medicine, nutrition, and training. The tips and information provided here will benefit new riders especially but will also be valuable for experienced mudders. If you feel that you must have the entire map series, you can order Worldguide products on CD; a link to Ziff-Davis Press (Your Personal Fitness Trainer CD) is also available.

Zia's Home Page
http://www-cse.ucsd.edu/users/zansari/

Zia Ansari has a mainly mountain bike–oriented home page that offers a couple of great services: the MTB Marketplace, where you can list your entire bike, frame, or components/accessories for sale (no road bike equipment allowed); and a comprehensive list of telephone numbers for mountain bike manufacturers. Available text documents include the rec.bicycles FAQ, the FAQ on suspensions, biking dictionaries, and instructions for various technical tasks, ranging from painting your bike to making your own brake boosters. Zia lists "cool MTB links" as well as some ski links.

Worldguide is a valuable online resource for any mountain biker.

Chapter 6

Racing

Whether you want to read the results of international races, view photos of top riders, check the calendar for upcoming races in your area, or get racing advice from great coaches and fellow riders in your category, you'll find it all on the Internet. This chapter reviews Web sites that dedicate themselves primarily to some aspect of racing (schedules, results, images, training, strategies) and lists the addresses for several major on- and off-road races. For regional racing schedules and news, check Chapter 13. Also, don't miss Steven Sheffield's Cycling the InfoBahn (Chapter 12), which serves as a central index to racing sites throughout the Internet (among other cycling links). Through many of these sites, you'll find links to professional (such as Banesto, EDS, and Saturn) and USCF team home pages, which vary widely in the amount of information they include. The Chevrolet-LA Sheriff team pages (http://www.infinet.com/) are especially well designed and informative (including cycling documents not specific to the team). Pages for European teams are usually in their native language. We've included two team (nonprofessional) Web sites—Team Internet and Team Working Title—as examples of how the Internet can be used to help promote and organize racing efforts.

Dictionary of Roadie Slang
http://searider.jpl.nasa.gov/~gms/text/slang.html
http://dutcu15.tudelft.nl/~geert/digicors/slang.htm

Geert van Oosterhout (original compiler) and Glenn Mitchell Shirtliffe received a lot of help putting together the Roadie Bike Slang Dictionary. You can learn what terms from "ate straw" to "Zoned" (and everything in between) mean in the context of road riding. Did you know Jaboffo or Jaboff was once used to refer to a Fred? A few words are explained in terms of the cyclist-type using them (road, mountain, track, trials, touring) with amusing results. You'll enjoy breezing through one of these sites to read what the roadies are talking about.

The Fabulous World of Cycling (by Eddy Merckx)
http://www-mount.ee.umn.edu/FCCC/fabulous-world-cycling.html

If you're ever looking for something to read on a rest day, you might want to stop by the Flat City Cycling Club's home page to read The Fabulous World of Cycling by Eddy Merckx (photographs by Alan Tonnoir). It's basically a collection of Merckx's comments on various photos of his career and personal reflections on the sport. Peter Bergner is putting photographs online as he is able, but you'll enjoy it no matter how far along he is.

Fat Tire Fotos
http://www.fattirefotos.com/

Mountain bikers will enjoy Matt Lanning's Fat Tire Fotos Web site, which includes up-to-date race results (very complete, with commentary and overall standings) and images from World Cup and NORBA races. The photographs are listed according to race and location and include cross country, downhill, circuit, and dual slalom events. Matt has the complete schedule for 1996 (and will, we hope, continue to post updated race schedules each year) and miscellaneous local photos and tidbits.

German Bicycle Racing Page
http://sunwww.informatik.uni-tuebingen.de:8080/sport/rad/rad.html

Peter Becker keeps track of the results for classic, World Cup, and stage races and the resulting rankings of international riders (only through 1994 at last check, though). What's especially nice is that all the information is available at Peter's site. You can check the team rosters for every professional road racing team. Other local files include the UCI doping list, the FICP scoring scheme and race calendar, pictures, two gearing tables (one metric), and a speed per pedal revolutions table. You can also read the full winners lists (all jerseys for the Tour de France) for more than a dozen tours and classics. He has many links to broader racing-related sites throughout the world and several German (cycling and noncycling) Web pages.

Karen Kurreck
ftp ftp.netcom.com/pub/ba/banders/cycling/

Brad Anders' FTP site includes pictures, race results, coaching strategies, and training tips, plus career notes about, training tips from, and photographs of World Time Trial Champion Karen Kurreck. You'll find coaching notes, hour record history, race calendars, bike-related software (especially useful for time trialists), wind tunnel tests results for wheels, and other information of interest to women racers and time trialists in particular.

Fat Tire Fotos is the place to go for professional photos and articles about mountain bike racing.

Major Taylor News and Results Service

http://www.go-interface.com/majtaylor/
Maj.Taylor@mymail.com

Jim Pailin (aka Maj.Taylor) operates Major Taylor News and Results Service, which delivers same-day professional race results and other news directly to your e-mail address. "Virtual" correspondents and reporters from all over the world provide same-day race commentary and results that are forwarded to subscribers in the United States, South Africa, Hong Kong, Australia, New Zealand, Germany, Denmark, Japan, and many other countries. If you only have an e-mail account, the service is invaluable. The fee for receiving racing and cycling news is very reasonable (quite a bargain, actually), and discounts are available for certain groups. If you're still uncertain, ask to see why Lance Armstrong, Paul Sherwen, Phil Liggett, and many other stars of the cycling world subscribe. (Be sure also to read Jim's story about the history of his service and Marshall "Major" Taylor himself on the next page.) Located at Cyber Cyclery, the Major Taylor's Results Archive (http://cyclery.com/racing/mtarchiv.html) is just that: a place you can read race results a day or two after they've been sent to subscribers. Bill Mitchell also includes coverage through Major Taylor on his Web site (http://econ-www.newcastle.edu.au/~bill/results.html).

Roger Marquis' Cycling Page

http://www.roble.com/marquis/

Roger Marquis keeps a tidy cycling page chock full of useful advice and links. Cyclists will learn how to prepare themselves and their bikes for competitive races with a wide range of useful articles, such as cycling psychology, competitive nutrition, descending skills, bike racing tactics, and seat and cleat adjustment. Roger's link to the Coaching mailing list archives likewise taps into a wealth of similar information.

National Collegiate Cycling Association (NCCA)

http://www.cse.psu.edu/~donadio/ncca-info/

The NCCA has a main Web page for the governing organization plus separate pages for each of the ten conferences. The main page has a handy What's New feature plus links to sites related to the NCCA, USCF, and NORBA. You'll be able to check championship results, find a license application or race entry form, learn how to put on a race, and memorize the "Top Ten Reasons Why I Didn't Train This Week" (and other racing humor). Sponsorship and fund-raising information is also available. Matt Donadio, an NCCA cyclist himself, takes care of the page and links you to several other cycling resources, including FTP, WWW, gopher, and newsgroup sites.

NCNCA Feed Zone

http://www.schmitzware.com/Phil/ncnca.html

Although this page serves members of the Northern California/Nevada Cycling Association, Phil Aaronson has provided plenty of information and links of interest to any cyclist involved in road, track, or cyclocross racing. Photographs and newsbytes are plentiful, and, in fact, the Feed Zone may evolve into an e-zine with articles on races, riders, and training for men and women from juniors to masters. Phil has links to interesting documents about racing—including his own technical note (i.e., lots of equations) about weight and climbing—software to help you train, many interesting Web sites (road, track, cyclocross, endurance), information about racing-related mailing lists, and race schedules throughout the United States and Canada.

Major Taylor's News & Results Service was not begun as a business or with any commercial intention. It was, quite frankly, an accident. More than 12 years ago I discovered I could get same-day cycling information from various sources, including news wires and, more importantly, other Internet users living in Europe. I began posting whatever I found to the Usenet newsgroup rec.bicycles.racing and kept this volunteer effort up for years. Over time, the name "Maj. Taylor" became recognized as a timely and reliable source of racing news about the professional peloton. Then, about 2 years ago, I began distributing the results via e-mail (still free of charge) when Internet growth began to affect the posting and reading of Usenet newsgroups. The service later became fee-based, with subscribers paying a small fee for an annual e-mail subscription.

Why the name Maj. Taylor? For those who don't already know, the business name "Maj. Taylor" pays homage to a great cyclist, Marshall "Major" Taylor. The real Major Taylor was a world-renown cyclist at the turn of the 20th century. In 1899, he won the world sprint championships and followed that with a U.S. National championship in 1900. Even so, one of his greatest fears was that he would be forgotten with the passage of time. Major Taylor was a black man, and as one of the very few black racers in bicycle racing almost 100 years later, I decided to honor his memory through the service. Just as Major Taylor was a pioneer in integrating professional sports, the cycling news service was a first in cyberspace. And now, like the real Marshall "Major" Taylor, the news service bearing his name is world renowned. I hope Major Taylor would be content with the fact that his name appears daily on computer screens around the world. He has not been forgotten.

Jim Pailin <aka Maj. Taylor>

Greg Nichols' Cycling Page
http://grumpy.usu.edu/~sl25z/index.html

Greg Nichols has a collection of excellent photographs of current and past road racers. He has shots of more than two dozen cycling stars (all <100 K GIF), including Eddy Merckx, Miguel Indurain, Greg Lemond, Steve Bauer, Sean Kelly, Gianni Bugno, Karen Kurreck, and many more. A few local photos and some good links round out the page. Be sure to check the Bike Racing Picture Archives (http://www.access.digex.net/~spatton/bike_pics/bike_pics.html), maintained by Wildman (aka Scott Lames).

Palmares of Professional Cyclists
http://www.handmadesw.com/~jessica/palmares.html

Joe Baily maintains an incredible collection of palmares for past and current professional road cyclists. You can check the racing careers of all the major and many less well known riders from around the globe. Joe has included interesting notes annotating the wins, major placings, and records set by these giants of the sport. He has organized the site so that no matter what you're looking for, it won't take long: yellow jersey wearers and stage winners of the most recent Tour de France (very nice for learning about those domestiques who get their day of glory); World Cup race winners; UCI ranking of riders; alphabetical listing of riders; alphabetical listing of retired riders; and new additions by date. Joe announces on rec.bicycles.racing when he's updated the page. He also includes links to Web pages with photographs of these riders and to current racing calendars and results postings.

Professional Teams
http://www.dds.nl/~michiel/fiets/ploegen.html

Although this site is in Dutch, you'll be able to understand the key information. Michiel van Loon has listed the team rosters and sponsors for every professional road team. He has photographs of several riders (presumably his favorites—and Nederland tops the page, of course) as well.

race-results@cycling.org
http://www.cycling.org/mailing.lists/race-results/

The race-results mailing list covers on- and off-road racing news for men and women, amateur and professional. You'll receive results from local criteriums to major international tours. World records are reported here, as are hotly contested finishes and other racing news. To subscribe, send a message to majordomo@cycling.org (`subscribe race-results`). The list's archives (maintained on VeloNet) are conveniently indexed by month and year (back to October 1994) and by topic (alphabetical subject list).

Raz's Velo-O-rama
http://wwwcsusm.edu/public/guests/rezell/razweb1.htm

Cycling writer John Rezell has launched Raz's Velo-O-rama, a central store-house of articles, photographs, and databases devoted to U.S. cycling. You'll find daily coverage and photos from major races, plus interesting reflections on the experience of attending the event. Special features, such as photo-finishes from each stage of the Tour of China (complements of FinishLynx Timing System), are often available as well. John describes how riders qualify for the Olympics, reviews training regimens, and interviews potential competitors. You'll certainly want to browse the Velo-O-rama Library, which includes profiles of amateur and professional racers (men and women) and coverage of the top races in the United States. Finally, he notes that he created Raz's Velo-O-rama in the "spirit of the Internet." He is happy to make this wealth of information and words freely available since he has "more information on US Cycling than [he] could ever use." He invites race promoters to use his rider profiles, photos, and features for their programs and club newsletter editors to download stories and columns.

Séamus Shortall's Irish Cycling Page
http://www.iol.ie/~sshortal/

Séamus Shortall maintains a nice, well-organized list of news about and results from races in Ireland and the United Kingdom (e.g., the Kingdom Cycle Series, Tour of Ulster, and Thwaites Brewery Grand Prix). He takes the excellent photos displayed throughout his Web pages by filming with his camcorder and then sampling the footage with his Videoblaster (he took the photo on the opening page with a camcorder in one hand and a 200 meter prime flag in the other). Irish riders will find contact information for the Federation of Irish Cyclists and other local information. A discriminating list of top-notch international cycling sites is also provided, as is a list of Irish-related Web pages.

> *For the past ten years, I've provided computerized scoring for bicycle stage races in Ireland and the United Kingdom. These events involve teams from all over the world and attract interest from cycle racing fans in the partici-pating countries and also from expatriates trying to keep up with local news. Traditionally, the scores are output on paper and are then transcribed by print and broadcast media. Using HTML pages automatically gener-ated from my scoring software, I can publish the results of these events cheaply, accurately, and instantaneously on a worldwide basis.*
> Séamus Shortall

Team Internet

http://www.sce.carleton.ca:80/rads/greg/team-internet/
ftp ftp.netcom.com:/pub/cy/cycling/team-internet
team-internet@cycling.org

Team Internet is an online bicycle racing team registered with the USCF, NORBA, and CCA (Canadian Cycling Association) and has members from all over the world. Cyclists living in remote areas not served by a bicycle club will appreciate the support and benefits available. You can use Team Internet as your club name on racing license applications, and your connections with team members to find training partners on the paved highways. You can purchase team clothing (very attractive—and copyrighted by designer and team member Thorns Craven) and keep up with how your mates are doing in their racing efforts through the Team Internet newsletter. You can also subscribe to the team-internet mailing list through VeloNet (send a sub-scribe team-internet message to majordomo@cycling.org) or request information about the team by sending e-mail to team-internet-request@cycling.org with the word INFO in the body of the message. The team Web site, maintained by Greg Franks, includes information on joining Team Internet, purchasing clothing, and contacting organizers, officers, and key team members, as well as useful racing links.

Bicycle racing is a team sport. But many weekend racers live in places where there is no local team to join. Frustration with this kind of situation led to the idea of organizing a racing team using the Internet as its point of contact. I first floated the idea on the rec.bicycles.racing in 1992, but it wasn't until 1994 that Kurt Sauer and I finally made the team a reality. 1995 was our first full year of existence, and although we are still working out exactly what the team is about, its growth to over 175 members in the United States, Canada, Europe, Australia, and Japan has far surpassed my expectations. We are currently affiliated with the national governing bodies in the U.S. and Canada, but I expect that we shall have affiliations in other countries as we continue to recruit members there.

Not all of our members race, but racing is the team's main objective. Because we are so spread out, our biggest challenge for the future will be to get members to compete together in the same races. I'm hopeful that as the team grows, so will the opportunities for a significant team presence at regional races. In the meantime, the great-looking team@internet jersey continues to attract attention on the road and at races and confirms to me that this experiment in cybercycling is already a success.

Colin Allen, http://team-internet.tamu.edu/cycling/

Team Working Title
http://galen.med.virginia.edu/~lal4e/

Team Working Title is a women's mountain bike racing team based in Virginia. You can visit their home page (maintained by Lee and Colleen) to see the team (photograph below by Chris McKenney) and their mascot Moto (probably not what you expect), the Mid-Atlantic mountain bike race schedule, and detailed information on trails in central Virginia. The sponsor section gives mini product reviews that are particularly useful for women looking for cycling equipment, and contact information for each company.

USCF Documents
ftp sail.stanford.edu/pub/les/

Les Earnest keeps a useful collection of United States Cycling Federation documents available for retrieval via FTP. You'll find entry forms, license applications, and rule books in a variety of formats, one of which you should be able to read with your available software. You'll probably meet Les on the rec.bicycles newsgroups, where he contributes statistics and advice.

World Media
http://www.worldmedia.fr/wm/velo/

This is the ultimate Tour de France site in terms of organization, and it's an important stop for anyone seeking racing information. You'll find everything from hourly updates to a place to ask individual riders or teams questions (answered online). If you'd prefer to read French, Spanish, Italian, German, or Russian reports, you can link up to international online news services to read stories written in these and other languages. Chief editor Gilbert Cattoire plans to add downloadable video, RealAudio, and other multimedia options. World Media also provides insightful commentary from professional cyclists such as Stephen Roche. Aside from live coverage (such as the Tour, Giro, Vuelta, and Tour of China), you'll find links to racing sites around the world.

Meet Team Working Title and many other racing teams online.

Major Races

You'll find consistent coverage of most major races and some lesser-known events. If a URL given below has been changed, you can search the Internet for specific races (Chapter 12) or go through one of the sites described earlier in this chapter (try World Media first for road, Fat Tire Fotos for mountain bike, and NCNCA Feed Zone for track). You might also visit Cycling the InfoBahn (Chapter 12). For regional races, check Chapter 13.

Collegiate Road Nationals (1996)
http://www.calpoly.edu/~rwarren/Wheelmen/Wheelmen.html

Cycle Messenger World Championships
http://www.lglobal.com/lgsites/cycle/cycle.html
http://www.sirius.com/~magpie/cmwc96/cmwc96.html

Cyclocross Racing (Japan)
http://www.yamanashi-med.ac.jp/~intern03/cross95-96/Cyclocross.homepageE

Dauphine Libere
http://www.elperiodico.es/   [in Spanish - go to Deportes]

Giro d'Italia
http://www.europe.ibm.com/getdoc/psmemea/underground/warpgiro/
http://www.energy.it/giro/   [in Italian]
http://sun.comm2000.it/rcs/

Goodwill Games Cycling Results
http://www.com/goodwill/cyccom.html

Grundig World Cup Races (1995)
http://www.quake.net/~baileyc/FTF/FatTireFotos.html

Iron Horse Bicycle Classic (Durango, CO)
http://web.frontier.net/SCAN/ihbc/ihbc.html

> *The velodromes-us mailing list was started to provide an easy way for the cycling tracks around the nation to communicate. Now the velodromes can easily share information about schedules, common problems, and news. Hopefully, by sharing ideas the nation's velodromes can work together to increase the number of riders and spectators coming to the tracks. The e-mail list should also prove a good way to talk to the people who are most active in promoting track racing and riding in the U.S. The list may become an information resource for people looking to build a velodrome in their community.*
>
> Casey Kerrigan, Northern California Velodrome Association

Milk Ras
http://www.iol.ie/~sshortal/ras95/overview.html

National Cycling Championships (1995)
http://www.eskimo.com/~cycling/national_95.html

National Off-Road Bicycleing Association Championships
http://www.tcinc.com/mtbike/vail.html
http://www.quake.net/~baileyc/FTF/FatTireFotos.html

Olympics (1996, cycling events)
http://www.atlanta.olympic.org/acog/sports/cycling/d-cycling.html

Powerbar International Women's Challenge
http://www.primenet.com/~krp/power.html

Thrift Drug Classic
http://www.cs.cmu.edu/afs/cs.cmu.edu/user/jdg/www/bike/thrift_drug_classic.html

Tour de France
http://franceweb.fr/letour/ [in French]
http://www.worldmedia.fr/wm/velo/tour/
http://www.best.com/~bikiebob/tdf95/index.html

Tour DuPont
http://www.firstunion.com/tourdupont/
http://www.lubricants.dupont.com/Tour95/Tour95.html
http://www.access.digex.net/~dforrest/tourhome.html/

Tour of China
http://www.www.access.digex.net/~dforrest/ktoc/ktochome.html

Twilight Criterium
http://monsterbit.com/twilightfresca.html

Vuelta a España
http://www.elperiodico.es/ [in Spanish - go to Deportes]
http://www.worldmedia.fr/wm/velo/vuelta/

World Media offers some of the best racing coverage online.

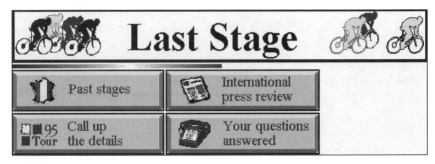

Chapter 7

Specialty Cycling

Road and mountain bikes aren't the only types of cycling with resources on the Internet. Tandem bicycles, unicycles, BMX bikes, recumbents, ham radio–equipped bikes, and all manner of human-powered vehicles have their place online. No matter what your cycling specialty is, you'll find others in cyberspace involved in the same aspect of the sport. This chapter reviews well-recognized alternative types of bicycles, such as tandems and recumbents, and some of the more niche markets, such as choppers and folding bicycles. You'll find discussion of most bikes in rec.bicycles.misc, including such useful documents as the Folding Bike FAQ by Steven Scharf. Don't forget to use the search engines described in Chapter 12 if you don't see any resources for your bicycle category here—more resources come online every week, and your group may have just signed on recently.

Bike Current

http://www.thesphere.com/bikecurrent/
bikecurrent@cycling.org

The Bike Current home page and mailing list (send `subscribe bikecurrent` message to majordomo@cycling.org) cover "issues concerning bicycles, electronics, and the combination of those two disciplines." You can check the archives on VeloNet and the Bike Current home page to learn more about what all this entails. A link to David Butcher's home page (http://www.los-gatos.scruznet.com/davidbu.html) will tell you about several pedal-powered projects. You'll also learn about Bike Mobile Hams of America, which invites anyone who uses their short-wave radio on a bike or other human-powered vehicle to join.

Bike Touring

http://pacificrim.net/~robert/bike.html

This site—"America at 10 miles per hour"—features a special cyclist and his special bicycle (duct tape features prominently). Robert Ashworth has an online book about his 4,000-mile bicycle trips across America. You can read through the entire 1991 journey (well worth the read) or jump to particular sections; the 1993 book is one long document (with exit links) focusing on the people he met. He intersperses travel experiences, history, and long-distance touring tips in concise, well-written prose. You can also view a slide show of photos he took. Other documents include a map of his 1991 journey and articles from local publications about his bike trips. Robert provides a link back to his main page and another (eventually) to Cyber Cyclery.

C.H.U.N.K. 666

http://www.reed.edu/~karl/chunk/

Karl Anderson maintains the homepage for C.H.U.N.K. 666, "a bicycle gang and temperance league" that uses uniquely designed "choppers" to get the same rush provided by alcoholic beverages. When you see the choppers, you'll understand. You can learn about a "wide-band chunkulation field" and view the Chunk fleet, made from an eclectic mix of spare parts and recycled items. You'll forgive them when photos of some missions, such as the "Flaming Wall of Death," are not available. If these thoroughly enjoyable photographs and stories convince you that you need a chopper, you can turn to the technical documentation for information on building your own chunkcycle.

International Human Powered Vehicle Association (IHPVA)

http://www.ihpva.org/
gopher.ihpva.org
ftp.ihpva.org

If you're interested in human-powered vehicles, check out the IHPVA home page. Cycling-related information and links abound, with an emphasis on recumbent bikes. You'll find a searchable index (but no articles) to back issues of Human Power: Technical Journal of the IHPVA, and can read some sample articles from the monthly newsletter, HPV News. The Recumbent FAQ is available here, as is information about Recumbent Cyclist News (DrRecumbnt@aol.com) and ultrariding. You can join the HPV mailing list at majordomo@ihpva.org (send the message `subscribe hpv`).

Ugglor was salvaged from the wreckage of an ancient alien spacecraft

No matter what type of bicycle you normally ride, set it aside and get on over to C.H.U.N.K. 666 as soon as your Web browser can get you there.

Magpie's Nest Home
http://www.strath.ac.uk:80/~cjbs23/

David Harper maintains a cozy nest on the Internet full of Web links for cyclists. You'll find locally at his site information about recumbent bikes, Aerobikes (a type of recumbent), Brompton Folding Bicycles, BROX zero-emission vehicles, the USA Short Wheel Base Pics, and the Glasgow Recumbent Club. David also provides links to several recumbent manufacturers (such as Easy Racers, Inc. and Future Cycles), the Moulton Bicycle Club, other human-powered vehicle pages, cycling magazines, and general cycling resources (such as VeloNet and Trento Bike Pages). Elsewhere on his page you'll find other interesting online places to visit, both throughout the United Kingdom and around the world.

Moulton Bicycle
http://www.warwick.ac.uk/~esrgq/moulton/moulton.html

You can learn all about the Moulton bicycle, its designer (Dr. Alex Moulton), and the Moulton Bicycle Club at a well-organized Web site maintained by Steve E. Michaels. You can read the history of the bicycle and the man, trace changes in design, read the Electronic Moulton Flyer and the Moulton FAQ, and check on upcoming rides and events.

Mountain Unicycling Index Page
http://www.msm.cam.ac.uk/CUCC/muni/munindex.html

"You ARE kidding?" is the apt introduction to the Mountain Unicycling Page by Jez Weston and others. Wait until you read about Jez's carbon fiber unicycle. Other delightful reading material includes "A fool and his muni are introduced" and "The complete idiot's guide to Mountain Unicycling." You'll learn how to go downhill and be "upwardly mobile" and read a "uni-que" perspective on competing in the MTB Pro Challenge two-day Mountain Unicycling Orienteering Event. How much more fun can you have on one wheel? Plenty, even if you just experience it through the MUni Pages.

You can check out the latest Moulton bicycle design (drawing by Nigel Sadler, editor of The Moultoneer) and many other specialty bikes on the Web.

National Bicycle League
http://www.microserve.net/nbl/

The National Bicycle League was formed in 1974 to take BMX competition from the backyard to the national and international level. The NBL home page includes information about what the organization does and what you need to do to get started in BMX racing. All the information necessary to develop that 200-rpm spin is available here. Cool photographs of BMXers in action, a list of 1995 events, and a comprehensive list of racing tracks around the country (with their schedules) round out this information-packed site, which is ably managed by Marty McCann.

New Jersey Bicycle Motorcross & Visions InfoLine
http://www.cnj.digex.net/~jmorgan

Jeff Morgan has dedicated his home page to BMX in New Jersey and to the racing career of his talented son Gregory. Jeff's page contains track race schedules for the New Jersey area and information about the Hunterdon BMX association (including an event schedule). This site also provides links to the NBL (National Bicycle League) and other BMX home pages. Jeff uses the page to invite sponsorship for Greg's riding career, and the information included speaks for itself on the worthiness of this goal.

In 1993, my son started BMX racing, and in 1994 we went to almost all the local tracks and the Grand Nationals. At the Grands, we learned that Greg didn't qualify because he didn't race any of the national races. With this knowledge, in 1995 we traveled throughout the northeast for races in Toronto, Cape Cod, Pittsburgh, and Long Island. During our travels, we kept meeting the same people at every race and got to know the National Bicycle League personnel. In '95 I also got an Internet SLIP account (I had already operated a 2-node BBS for six years) and started browsing the Net for bike organizations. I tried to learn about the places we were going to be racing but found very little information. I also learned that no electronic BMX publications were available. I thought a Web page might be a good way to promote my son's racing career. It started out as a picture and a plea for money but has grown to become one of the best-known pages on the sport of BMX and is listed in both Yahoo and Lycos. My main drive now is to make the sport of BMX racing better known for the quality of people who race and to eliminate some of the myths like, "BMXers... Yeah, they're tomorrow's Hell's Angels."

Jeff Morgan

Nomadic Research Labs

http://microship.ucsd.edu/

Steven Roberts, "a technomad for the past 11 years," and Faun Skyles have set up a Web site for Nomadic Research Labs. You'll be able to read descriptions of and tales related to his vehicles (Behemoth, Winnebikeo, Microship), learn how to order books describing his ventures, see where he'll be speaking next, check what's available at his garage sale (how does a "105-speed computerized recumbent bike" sound?), and use his links to other miscellaneous sites for mobile computing and human-powered vehicles.

Recumbents and Technomadics

http://fred.net/kathy/benttech.html

As part of her home page, Kathy Bilton has a Recumbent and Technomadics page written as prose, with hypertext links throughout the paragraphs (instead of a list of bulleted choices). You'll find a recumbent bikes FAQ, links to other 'Bent Folks with home pages, images of recumbents and other unusual vehicles, and ties to human-powered vehicle sites.

Tandem Page

http://www-acs.ucsd.edu/home-pages/wade/tandem.html

Wade Blomgren's home page for the tandem@hobbes mailing list includes information about joining the list (send `subscribe tandem` *your name* message to listserv@hobbes.ucsd.edu), and what to expect from it, plus an impressive list of tandem links. The most important link for new or expectant tandem riders is to the list archives site, which includes many FAQs and important advice and information. You can also get to Wade's list of Cycling Related Links, which include general bicycle sites, commuting information, triathlon pages, and more tandem spots as well as cycling stuff local to San Diego. The tandem@hobbes list logo, shown below (and reproduced on stickers, water bottles, and jerseys), was designed by Anne Summers with help from Jim Becker and other subscribers.

The tandem@hobbes mailing list and Web documents are invaluable resources for new tandem users and experienced riders alike.

Tandem Specific Info
http://blueridge.infomkt.ibm.com/bikes/text/Tandems/Tandems.html

 As part of his comprehensive set of cycling Web pages, Steve Ciccarelli offers a long list of tandem resources and links. Much of his information is from the tandem@hobbes archives, including several FAQs (overview, new riders, buying a tandem, more experienced tandem riders, glossary, etc.). Steve has gone through the tandem@hobbes mailing list archives to put some of the best postings (organized by subject heading) locally on his site. He also has information about the Tandem Club of America and a rally schedule.

Tandem Tour
http://www.teleport.com/~elemon/biketour.html

Eric and Melissa LeMoine have chronicled their tandem tour from Portland, Oregon, to Jasper, Alberta. They include text and pictures about their training rides, a map of their route (GIF), information about how they packed for the trip (very detailed lists with lots of good tips), and a series of pages that cover each leg of the journey (described by start and end points). Coverage of the tour has photographs and a travelogue that addresses everything from riding conditions to interesting facts about sights along the way.

Unicycling Home Page
http://unicycling.org
ftp ftp.mcs.kent.edu/pub/unicycling

Beirne Konarski (with Ken Fuchs) has set up the Unicycling Home Page to support and inform new and experienced unicyclists alike. You'll find a FAQ on unicycling, instructions on learning to ride a unicycle, a classified section for buying and selling unicycles, fun things to try on your unicycle, a list of e-mail addresses and home pages for fellow unicyclists, a unicycle photo album, and many more one-wheeled resources. You can even watch a computer animation clip of a unicycle, Red's Nightmare, and look at Bungee Jumping on the Unicycle ("This will give you a goal in life"). Of course, Beirne provides updated links to scores of Internet unicycling resources.

> *The Unicycling Home Page covers a variety of aspects of unicycling. Features include learning to ride, learning advanced skills, buying a unicycle, games like unicycle hockey, and pictures and animations. The page also includes ways to interact with other unicyclists through rec.sport.unicycling, a roster of unicyclists, a list of clubs, and information on unicycle meets.*
>
> Beirne Konarski

Chapter 8

Social and Safety Issues

Many aspects of living with bicycles are discussed online. Advocacy groups have taken full advantage of the global audience and use the Internet, BBSs, and commercial services to broadcast their message and to organize their public efforts. America Online's BikeNet (Chapter 2) hosts several cycling organizations, and Outside Online (Chapter 9) provides Web access to many of these same groups. Commuters will find plenty of assistance and camaraderie online. You'll also find help keeping safe, keeping your bike in good working condition (read rec.bicycles.tech, too)—and keeping your bike! The rec.bicycles.soc newsgroup covers all of these issues and many more topics related to bicycles in society (court cases, cars, children, etc.), so you should check in there for information not explicitly listed in this chapter.

Bicycle
http://mark.allyn.com/bicycle.html

As part of his home page, Mark Allyn provides an extensive document with tips on commuting, descriptions of gadgets he uses, suggestions for handling commuting logistics, and an overview of his own commuting experience. Mark has survived "three New England winters...three years in car craving California [and] ten years here in Seattle" without a car, so he knows what he's talking about. He explains his Ham Radio Commuter Bike separately.

Bicycle Commuting
http://www.spies.com/~ceej/Distractions/bikes.html

C.J. Silverio has a terrific section on bicycle commuting as part of his home page. He recommends checking the rec.bicycles FAQ (and provides a link) for everything you need to know about bicycles and restricts his own coverage to Getting on that bike, Spiffing up your bike, Choosing a route, Coexisting with cars, and Getting more information [about commuting]. Also included are links to a few select international and regional cycling resources.

> *I have survived without a car for 18 year in car culture America. I would like to show everyone out there that it is possible and is a great joy! It's not the money that I save by not having a car; it is the independence that turns me on. It's just lots of fun! Best thing is breezing past cars stuck in traffic and waving at them!*
> Mark Allyn

Bicycle Federation of Australia

http://www.ozemail.com.au/~bicycle/

The Bicycle Federation of Australia is "a nonprofit organization of major bicycle advocacy groups in Australia, dedicated to promoting cycling for transport and recreation, thus serving the best interests of the community and environment." The Federation publishes Australian Cyclist, and you can learn about subscribing and contributing to the magazine at this site. You'll find addresses for all of the member organizations (scattered around the continent) and links to their home pages (most if not all should be available by now). Be sure to thank Graeme Lothringer for maintaining this service.

Bicycle Helmet Safety Institute (BHSI)

http://www.bhsi.org
helmets@bhsi.org

The Bicycle Helmet Safety Institute is an advocacy program of the Washington Area Bicyclist Association, the United States' oldest regional bicycle advocacy group. Volunteers in this program serve on the ASTM and ANSI bicycle helmet standard committees, and you can see their ambitious plans in one of the documents on the Web site. You'll also find A Consumer's Guide to Bicycle Helmets, information on bicycle helmet standards (ASTM, ANSI, Snell, and others), crash stories, a list of mandatory helmet laws (full text and summary sheets), a compendium of helmet statistics, specific unique advice (large head, lice, children, etc.), the BHSI newsletter (with extensive coverage of industry and legislative news), and much more. Randy Swart manages this terrific site, which is chock full of useful documents and advice (and delightful illustrations, such as the one below, by Nancy Jennis Olds).

The Bicycle Helmet Safety Institute maintains an excellent consumer's guide and will keep you informed about helmet standards and statistics.

Bicycle Parking
http://tdc-www.harvard.edu/bicycle/bike.parking.html

Doug Mink of Mass Bike maintains a page with bicycle parking laws for
Cambridge (MA), Santa Cruz (CA), and Denver (CO)—more may be
available now. You'll find appropriate excerpts from the actual city code. If
you're in Pennsylvania, you might want to check the section on Bicycling
Law in Pennsylvania available on John Greiner's Pittsburgh Bicycling Home
Page (http://www.cs.cmu.edu/afs/cs.cmu.edu/user/jdg/www/bike/law_pa.html).

Bike'alog
http://www.bikealog.com

The Bike'alog Web page (spun by Dan Nguyenphuc) is an online catalog of
specifications, contact information, industry news, and dealer lists for just
about every bicycle manufacturer. You can look at a picture of the bike, check
all the components and options, and compare prices (suggested retail given).
Anyone looking for a bike will find this service invaluable. You can also visit
the Bike Shop of the Week, which is a link to a selected online retail store. (If
you know the *type* of bike you want but not the manufactuer, try Doug
Bogia's page, which organizes links back to Bike'alog according to bicycle
type, at http://acsl.cs.uiuc.edu/~bogia/Bikes/index.html—also check here
for updated links if the main Bike'alog site moves, which it might according
to Dan).

Bike Lights FAQ
http://www.bath.ac.uk/~bspahh/bikelights/lights.html

Andrew Henry has prepared what he modestly calls a "mini FAQ on bicycle
lights" but that is actually an exhaustive coverage of this critical safety topic.
Whether for your evening training rides, daily commute, or Race Across
America plans, this Bike Lights FAQ will answer just about any question you
might have about being seen on your bike at night.

Book of Advice
http://www.mainelink.net/~cymbop/bike.html

Brad Miele, a bike mechanic in Maine, answers technical questions online,
though you'll probably find all the answers you need in his Book of Advice.
Brad organizes common questions he's received in the past according to
repair or maintenance area: Bottom Brackets and Cranks; Brakes; Components (shifters, derailleurs, etc.); Drivetrain (chains, cogsets, etc.); Forks
(mostly suspension); Frames; and Wheels. He gives succinct, straightforward
answers in a manner that demonstrates his respect for fellow cyclists and his
knowledge of bicycle maintenance.

Critical Mass
http://www.chu.cam.ac.uk/home/tgs1001/cm.html

Critical Mass, "Active campaigning against the car culture…", has a Web site to inform anyone interested in this advocacy group about its mission, its chapters throughout the world, its lingo, and its activities. You'll also learn Critical Mass terminology, such as "corking," "organized coincidence," and "Going to Mass." The site is full of Critical Quotes from Critical Mass participants that will give you unique insight into what the group is about. Links are provided to several pages with Critical Mass information (you can read Critical Mass Times through the DC site at http://www.gallaudet.edu/~kjcole/Bike/CriticalMass.html). You can reach Critical Mass via e-mail at carmagedon@aol.com as well.

Green Action UK
http://www.envirolink.org/orgs/greenaction/cycle.html

Among the many environment-friendly databases available at the Green Action of Glasgow page (created by David Marsh), you'll find the cycling pages a convenient collection of useful information. There is a brief description, contact information, and, if available, a link to Bike Culture Quarterly, Cycle Campaign Network, Cyclists' Touring Club, European Cyclists' Federation, Glasgow Cycling Campaign, National Bike Week, and Sustrans (Paths for People). More than three dozen local (United Kingdom) groups are represented as well. You'll be able to check on current national and local policies for transporting bicycles on trains in the United Kingdom, including a useful list of individual rail line policies and bike-friendly areas throughout the country.

I live 7 km north of downtown Melbourne, Australia, almost on top of the Upfield Bikepath. I use my bike at work and for general transport, about 100 km per week. I ride a comfortable, speedy, Reynolds 531 custom-built tourer from Ian, at Christie Cycles. My riding style varies from gung ho to cautious aggression to taking it easy. (I am not as abusive as I used to be since I gave a motorist the finger and he tried to run me off the road.) Bikes are a lot safer than cars once you learn to read traffic and take a few precautions. Traffic is a challenge, not something to be afraid of. Whistle near pedestrians if you have to alert them. It's not as confronting as a bell (I whistle a lot while riding anyway). What I Dream About Whilst Riding: The Great Australian Bike Movie.

Nicholas Elliot,
Bicycle Transport Coordinator, Moreland City Council

National Bicycle Greenway
http://www.mochinet.com/cycle/nbg/

The National Bicycle Greenway seeks to "promote the coast to coast, multi-use transportation and recreational bicycle trail." At the Greenway Web page (maintained by Cycle America), you can learn how the group is going to make this happen, see what they're already doing, meet the folks involved, and join the effort yourself. You can also read articles on commuting and enjoying a car-free lifestyle, and reviews of bicycles and equipment, such as a test ride of the BikeE recumbent bike.

One Less Car
http://olc.ismcan.com/
gopher olc.ismcan.com port 70
416-480-0147 (up to 28.8 bps)

Peter Kroiker operates the One Less Car Web page, gopher server, and BBS, which means that anyone with a computer and a modem can take advantage of the cycling information and software available here. If you live in Toronto, you can't afford not to contact One Less Car through one of these methods. Even if you live elsewhere, you'll still find plenty of useful information. Several aspects of cycling, from commuting to tandems, are covered here. The gopher server, which mirrors the BBS, includes current and back issues of the Cyclometer (Toronto City Cycling Committee newsletter), reports and surveys on cycling around Toronto, bike graphics, and software (gear ratio and spoke length calculators, training logs, etc.). Local organizations featured here include the Toronto City Cycling Committee, Metro Cycling Committee, Metro By Cycle, and Toronto Off Road Cyclists. Web links to Internet cycling resources are organized as Canadian and the Rest of the World.

Pedestrian/Bikeways Committee
http://www.nd.edu/~ktrembat/www-bike/

"WARNING! The Surgeon General warns that bicycle commuting is addictive and may be beneficial to your health." You'll learn how to feed that addiction using articles (mainly from Bicycling Magazine), advice, and links with a common commuting theme maintained by Kern Trembath. Potpourri includes lots of miscellaneous tips, such as adjusting helmet fit, adjusting seat position, riding with a child, and much more. Local information for the Notre Dame/Saint Mary's College area is also available, as are other Indiana cycling sites (Michiana Bicycle Association, the Northern Indiana Mountain Bike Association, the Indiana Bicycle Coalition). You'll find cycling information for the entire United States offered through an interactive map, and the Indiana Bicycle Coalition offers current contact information for all members of the U.S. Congress.

Snell Memorial Foundation
http://www.emory.edu/WHI/snell.home.html

The Snell Memorial Foundation has devoted its Web site to explaining how helmets are certified for various sports and listing helmets that Snell has approved. You can also read more about the foundation itself and transfer to World Health Organization Helmet Initiative.

Spoke Length Calculators
http://www.roble.com/marquis/spolen11.bas
gopher://sisgopher.ismcan.com:70/1olcgo-p.70
gopher://draco.acs.uci.edu:1071

You'll find many spoke length calculators available online. Roger Marquis offers the code for a QuickBasic program, or you could download freeware and shareware calculators from the One Less Car or rec.bicycles gophers. Richard Wurdack formerly provided an interactive Web-based calculator (http://www.cyberspace.com/~richtw/sl.cgi), but it has moved or vanished.

Stolen Bike Registry
http://www.nashville.net/cycling/stolen.html

Andrew Warner has developed an excellent online resource for anyone who owns a bike: the Stolen Bike Registry (he also maintains a database of speed traps). You can preregister your bike, add the information on your stolen bike to the registry, or search the registry to see if a suspicious bike has been reported. You'll find many links from cycling pages all over the world to the Stolen Bike Registry, which is part of the Nashville Net Cycling Home Page (http://www.nashville.net/cycling/), a worthy place to visit on its own.

Stolen bikes & the Internet? Yeah, I know they seem to fit together about as well as power tools and spam. Though it never would have been possible a few years ago, the Net has grown to accommodate thousands of niche services. The Stolen Bike Registry has three major components: the stolen submit, the preregister submit, and the database. The two submits are nearly identical, the only difference being the preregistration doesn't have any fields about where or when it was stolen. The information from the forms is interpreted by a PERL script and entered into the database. I'm the only one who sees the preregistration database—I wouldn't want people to use it to steal bikes. Every few days, I read through the stolen entries and add the new ones to the end of the list. The more people participate, the more successful the registry will be, so please stop by.

Andrew Warner

Tech Tips

gopher gopher.millsaps.edu/11gopher_root_foodserv:[techinfo]
http://www.millsaps.edu/~kingst/bike.html

Steve King multitasks his Web site to provide everything from racing results to Millsaps Bike Club info, but his Tech Tips gopher server fills a tremendous need (see figure on page 29). You'll find guidelines for checking bike fit, buying bicycles and components, calibrating cyclometers, truing wheels, and adjusting and servicing many parts and systems. There's also a list of technical support numbers and information about frame materials, theft prevention, and part dimensions. You'll find links to Steve's Health and Fitness Tips and to Bike Handling and Training Skills, both of which are offered through the Web site and gopher servers and both of which are well worth the visit.

Winter Cycling

http://mudhead.uottawa.ca/~pete/bike.html

Pete Hickey shows and tells you how he manages to keep commuting on his bike during Canadian winters. You'll get to see pictures of Pete with his face frozen and of Pete's bike covered with snow and ice (see below). You can read his recommendations for equipment, clothing, riding technique, stopping (riding into a snowbank is one option), and dealing with several minor details, such as frozen locks. He also gives tips on eating a popsicle on the road. For more winter tips, you may want to check Vincent Chen's page at http://www.ualberta.ca/~vccheng/ (Vince is also keeper of the MTB FAQ) or join the icebike mailing list (maintained through VeloNet).

If you're planning to do any winter commuting, be sure to visit Pete Hickey's Web site for advice.

World Health Organization Helmet Initiative
http://www.emory.edu/WHI/home.html

Directed by Philip Graitcer, the World Health Organization (WHO) has established a comprehensive set of pages describing the goals, work, and progress of its worldwide effort to promote the use of motorcycle and bicycle helmets. You can read detailed and thoughtful articles in Headlines, the official newsletter of the WHO Helmet Initiative (jointly published with the Emory Center for Injury Control and the Centers for Disease Control and Prevention) and several other documents relating to helmet laws, injury prevention, and emergency services.

The Snell Memorial Foundation and the World Health Organization Helmet Initiative are conveniently located at the same Web site.

I started my Web page, not only to provide a Canadian mail-order bike catalog running exclusively off the WWW (no print catalogs available) but also to provide a source for technical tips and tricks for the avid mechanic as well as a source of info for the rider looking to trick out his bike in a personalized way.

Kristan Roberge
KMR Cycles Online http://infoweb.magi.com/~kroberge/kmrtop.html

Chapter 9

Magazines and Media

The Internet is rapidly becoming an electronic newsstand. In fact, you can check out the official Electronic Newsstand (http://www.enews.com/) for information about hundreds of print magazines. However, you'll probably be more interested in reading the online magazines (often just called 'Zines or e-zines on the Net) at their various Web sites. Most offer several sample articles plus the table of contents, topics covered in back issues, subscription information, forms for e-mailing comments, and links to other cycling sites. A few are entirely online (no print version); these are generally volunteer efforts rather than commercial enterprises. You'll also find a few sites maintained by multimedia corporations, such as ESPNet. Be sure to read Chapter 2 for coverage of Bicycling Magazine Online, which offers an extensive electronic version of its print magazine plus many additional services and benefits. Finally, you'll find the Endurance Training Journal and other training document compilations (but not really e-zines) in Chapter 10.

220
http://www.twotwenty.com/~twotwnty/
TwoTwoZero@aol.com

The initial online offering of this triathlete magazine is very restricted: an online form for subscribing and sending comments, a description of the print version, and telephone numbers for subscribing in the United States, the United Kingdom, and France. You might want to check to see if they have added to their Web site any sample articles from 220 or links to tri-related online sites (neither available at last check).

Balance Magazine
http://tito.hyperlink.com/balance/whole.htm
balance@hyperlink.com

Balance Magazine covers topics in fitness, health, and nutrition. As with print magazines, you'll find editorials, feature stories, news updates, an events calendar, product information, and quick tips. Back issues are available as well. Fitness, lifestyle (diet, health, stress), therapy (sports injuries, massage, treatments), forums (reader's comments, editorials, quizzes), international events, and featured people, places, products, and trends receive their own pages. Articles are thorough and include cross links among related topics. Balance offers a free e-mail reminder service so that you know when the magazine has been updated (the first day of every month). Editor Howard Jardine has done a great job ensuring that Balance lives up to its name.

Big Ring Magazine

http://www.nashville.net/~xizang/bigring.html
ftp ftp.telalink.net/users/x/xizang/web/
xizang@nashville.net

Steven Howard, editor of Big Ring "the Zine," has been working hard to
expand the features offered in this online mountain biking magazine. You'll
find articles describing various bikes, trails in the Nashville area (including
technical ability needed, length, directions, places to rest, etc.), nutrition,
maintenance (such as how to rebuild your Rock Shox Mag 20 or Mag 21 and
other air/oil shocks), and indoor training. You can contact the authors to
express your opinions on their work or ask questions, and readers are invited
to submit their own articles. Steve gives you the option of subscribing by e-
mail, retrieving individual issues via FTP, or reading the current issue on the
Big Ring Web page. Back on his own home page, Steve includes several
(mainly mountain bike) cycling links.

Bike Culture Quarterly (BCQ)

http://www.cyclery.com/open_road
bcq@primenet.com
OpenRdUSA@aol.com

Published by Open Road Ltd. in Britain, BCQ "reports on the latest techno-
logical advances" but focuses on the "art, culture, and human interest side of
cycling." Open Road USA is an expanded version of BCQ that includes news
and commentary on cycling in North America. You'll find commentaries,
photo essays, art, humor, and fiction in the print version; the online BCQ
offers sample articles for your enjoyment. You can also preview the BCQ
Encyclopedia, an annual book featuring an equally wide range of unique
cycling products. The printed book is divided into Recumbents, Classics,
Family Bikes, Trikes, Portable Bikes, and Accessories (full-color photo,
description, and BCQ opinion of each). The Web site provides you with a
nice selection of sample entries to give you a flavor of the full publication.

*You'll find useful mountain biking information in Big Ring the Zine whether you
live in Nashville or Nashua.*

Crank

http://www.resource.com/crank/welcome.html
dshust@resource.com

Crank is a dynamic MTB e-zine with a fun interface (it's worth dropping by to see the cartoon headers) and solid content. Rather than publishing "issues," Crank continually adds new content, archiving older articles. In the Rantilever section, you'll learn what's on the mind of The Crankster. The Test Tube gives "the straight spoke on new stuff," while the Patch Kit covers practical tips on getting the most out of your biking experience. Crank also offers Reader Rigs, "a kind of 'internet stable' for our readers' trusted steeds." You're invited to describe your bike and send a picture. Other features include the Ride Guide, the Skidule, the Trophy Room, and Chain Links (there's a separate link to Riddler Games). Throughout the site, you can leave comments, requests, and questions whenever you read something that motivates you to respond. Editor Dan Shust has done a fantastic job setting up Crank and keeping it alive and kicking with terrific information.

Cyber Cyclist

http://hyperlink.com:9000/bike
cybercycle@hyperlink.com

Editor Pete Hodgetts brings all aspects of cycling—road, off-road, track— together in his monthly online magazine Cyber Cyclist. You'll find news from the offline world of cycling as well as NetNews relevant to bike aficionados. Features range from specialized (downhill, mud riding, volcanic trails) to general interest (shaving your legs, bikie cafés). New technology is explained in refreshingly understandable prose, and product reviews go beyond the latest aluminum bike or suspension fork to include apparel, energy drinks, aero wheels, and other specialty items. Advocacy issues are discussed here, and touring information from all over the world abounds. Just about anyone will appreciate the Cycling Dictionary and similar resources.

Crank started out kinda on a goof and within a couple weeks, I was getting hits and e-mail from all over the world: the U.S., Australia, Japan, Canada, the UK—even the Czech Republic. As I write this, about 2,000 people visit Crank every week. They have ideas they want to share, products they want reviewed, bikes they'd like the world to see, etc. A lot of them just want to say hi and drop a word of encouragement. The Web has allowed me to do something I could never have achieved through traditional methods. It's pretty cool. Remember to Crank!

Dan Shust, Editor/Publisher/Designer/Illustrator/Photographer/Writer

Cycling Plus

http://www.futurenet.co.uk/outdoors/cyclingplus.html
djoyce@futurenet.co.uk

Editor Dan Joyce brings the print version of Cycling Plus online as "a cyclists' café." The main Web page is well organized and compact. Features are at the top of the list (nutrition, technical tips, new bike technology, sports medicine, training and racing strategies, cycling and the Internet, etc.), followed by reviews, back issues, subscription information, advertiser information, and links to other cycling sites. When appropriate, articles have links to other sites on the Web, and the graphics do not bog down the magazine too much—a text-based reader will do fine here. Although produced in the United Kingdom, Cycling Plus will appeal to cyclists anywhere in the world.

Cycling Science

http://s2.com:80/cycsci/
penner@ix.netcom.com

Cycling Science is a quarterly magazine "dedicated to both the science and performance of technical cycling." You'll find serious information here written at a professional level—no quick tips or popular press–type feature stories. You'll find papers such as "Effect of Oral Creatine Supplementation on Power Output and Fatigue During Bicycle Ergometry" (didn't work). At this Web site, you can read abstracts of articles from current and back issues as well as the subscription details. You can read sample stories at Cyber Cyclery (http://www.cyclery.com/cycling_science/index.html).

Dirt Rag

http://www.cyclery.com/dirt_rag/index.html
DirtRag1@aol.com

As the editors and publisher Maurice Tierney say, "Dirt Rag is a nonglossy magazine written by and for real mountain bikers." The print version includes Places to Ride, Eats, Trail Mix, Land Access News, Event Reports, Dirt Stuff, and much more. Online you'll find sample articles, detailed guidelines for submissions (instructions and payment schedule for each section or column), and order forms for back issues and subscriptions.

Dirt Rag is written by and for mountain bikers on- and offline.

ESPNet

http://espnet.sportszone.com/editors/other/
http://espnet.sportszone.com/editors/selsports.html
espnet.sportszone@starwave.com

Whether you'll find anything on ESPN's SportsZone depends on what cycling events are currently being held. Major races, such as the Tour de France, get a lot of coverage, but lesser-known races are not likely to appear here. However, the Tour coverage is excellent, including leaderboard, stage maps and results, daily wrap-ups, history (past champs, multiple winners, winners by country), multimedia coverage (photo, video, and audio clips), team information and sponsors, the schedule for televised coverage, and a place to ask questions or leave comments about ESPN's coverage of the Tour.

GearHead Magazine

http://www.gearhead.com/
http://gearhead.com/
GearHedMag@aol.com

"GearHead is the first *Organic* mountain bike magazine." That is, no print version exists—only the dynamic online Web site headed by editor-in-chief David Schloss. The Saddlebag contains product reviews, while Features covers everything from how Tom Ritchey designs new tires to tips for waxing your chain. You'll find new product announcements on the Spec Sheet and "best-of-the-best" bike dealers on the Shop List. Of course, the Master Link attempts to keep up with the growing number of online cycling resources. GearHead also offers late-breaking news, letters, and editorials.

Inside Triathlon Online

http://www.insidetri.com/tri/
insidetri@aol.com

Inside Triathlon Online offers a race calendar, table of contents for the print version, merchant information, links to other triathlon sites on the Web, the usual magazine information (mail, subscription, credits, etc.), and Training with Dave Scott, including "a six week crash course for half Ironman and Ironman athletes." The Table of Contents section also includes a sample article and race results. You'll need to turn on your browser's graphics option.

At GearHead, "the Squeaky Wheel [editors and readers] gets the grease."

La Bicicletta
Bici da Montagna
http://www.nexus.it/cyclingitaly
bici.it@nexus.it
bdm.it@nexus.it

Italy's leading cycling publications, La Bicicletta (road) and Bici da Montagna (MTB) are online for all the world to read. All the Italian-speaking world, that is. It appears that you'll find full-text articles and columns plus cycling news. (Instructions and notes about the page are in English.) You can also check on Italian bikes and components using an index (arranged alphabetically) to select the company of choice.

Mountain Biking UK
http://www.futurenet.co.uk/outdoors/mbuk.html
brant@cix.compulink.co.uk

Brant Richards, technical editor of Mountain Biking UK, "Britain's bestselling bike magazine," brings some of the best features of the print version online. The articles are detailed and illustrated, and should prove useful to bikers at any level of expertise. Features include Grime Time Clinic (technical queries), Grime Time (maintenance), and Group Test (reviews and ratings). You can check what's available in current and back issues (table of contents with brief description of each piece); the Events Calendar restricts itself to the United Kingdom. You'll find the same links, advertiser information, and organization list as in Cycling Plus and MTB Pro plus a subscription form.

MTB Pro
http://www.futurenet.co.uk/outdoors/mtbpro.html
mtbpro@futurenet.co.uk

MTB Pro, "Britain's most stylish mountain biking magazine" really is "100% mountain biking." You'll find reviews of bikes and components, tutorials for improving your bike-handling skills, the latest racing and industry news, interviews with top riders (such as Tom Ritchey, the ubiquitous John Tomac, and Missy Giove) and descriptions of trails throughout the United Kingdom. The Web site includes the table of contents for current and back issues and a nice selection of feature stories to read online. In fact, MTB Pro has one of the best designs for presenting feature articles: you read through each section on a separate page and can quickly hop back to the main page or elsewhere in the article using a handy index at the bottom. Because the articles are well illustrated, this method avoids lengthy delays that would otherwise be caused by loading the entire article all at once. In review articles, you can "Skip to the MTB Pro overall verdict" as well. As usual, you'll find plenty of links, advertiser information, and subscription options.

MBElectro

http://mbelectro.com/mbelectro/
mbelectro@earthlink.net

MBElectro is the electronic version of Rodale Press' Mountain Bike Magazine. Regular visitors can check MB Flash, a news service that is updated on Sundays. Under Entertainment, you'll find Mountain Bike Magazine Preview, Hug the Bunny, The Best of Trailhead, and Dirt Dish (race results). Swag City includes bike and product reviews, with a searchable archive to help you find the item you need. MB Trails is an interactive section where you can list your favorite trail and search the Backcountry Index to off-road, multiday adventures. As usual, there's a place for Feedback (rants and comments as well as questions posed to Uncle Knobby), credits and contacts, subscription and contribution information, and links to other bike sites. MBElectro editor Dan Koeppel has done a great job getting this fine magazine online.

Outside Online

http://web2.starwave.com/outside/online/index.html
contact.outside@starwave.com

Outside Online is much more than an electronic version of its print magazine: you'll find forums, late-breaking news, travel resources, advocacy advice, and the Outside Store—plus great cycling information. Major cycling events from the Tour de France (on- and off-road versions) to the Race Across America (RAAM) to the Gatorade Ironman receive coverage, and basic fitness and training topics are also featured. The editors have interviewed cycling celebrities, including none other than Greg Lemond, who answered online questions related to cycling in general, his career, the Tour de France, and his future plans. You can post your own question or read the archives later; online questions answered by Missy Giove, Juli Furtado, and Leigh Donovan should also be available by now. The magazine announces these events in advance on the rec.bicycles newsgroups. Outside Online's links will help you plan your next cycling excursion, with ties to maps, weather updates, national parks, travel services, environment fact sheets, and a smattering of cycling pages all over the Web. Advocacy (including U.S. and international bicycling organizations) and commercial links are also provided.

If you like Bicycling Magazine on AOL, don't miss MBElectro on the Web.

Oz on Dirt
http://www.usyd.edu.au/~rsaunder/welcome.html

Robert Saunders and Scott Taylor update this new Aussie mountain biking e-zine weekly with news and views on the dirt scene down under. You'll be able to follow mountain biking in all its forms and take advantage of the Oz on Dirt technical tips, product reviews, image archive, and much more.

SINGLE TRACK The Mountain Bike Magazine
http://www.amazing.com/cycling/sthome.html
singletr@amazing.cinenet.net

SINGLE TRACK The Mountain Bike Magazine brings online the usual collection of trails and rides, technical and riding tips, product reviews, calendars, classifieds, and interviews. Much of the trail and event information is local to southern California; the race section spans the globe. Editor Bradford Young invites you to submit editorials and comments on his work in progress, which had just come online as we went to press.

Tandem Magazine
http://www.efn.org/~tandem/
Tandem@efn.org

Tandem Magazine offers a slick Web site designed for both graphical and text browsers for duet-minded riders. To help you decide whether to subscribe to the quarterly print version (form available online), the staff has posted lists of the contents from back issues and provided a sampling of articles scattered throughout the site. You'll also find information on tandem dealers and related commercial services, sponsors of Tandem Magazine, and a list of tandem clubs. Classified ads are available as well. You can transfer to several tandem-related Web sites, check a calendar of tandem events, view pictures and descriptions of vintage tandems and triplets, and read product reviews and tandem road tests. Editor Greg Shepherd welcomes your opinions (try the Yada section), reports about tandem events (photos are welcome), and suggestions for Tandem Magazine.

Tandem Magazine online offers much more than articles and ads.

t@p online
http://www.taponline.com/tap/extreme/mtbike.html
bike@taponline.com

College and university students will want to ride by t@p online, which covers just about every collegiate area of interest. The MTB section offers an interesting mix of features, fun, and answers. CyberBikers tell their tales of offline, off-road riding and online adventures meeting other folks. Answers include those given by Richard Hayter (questions submitted via e-mail) and t@p product reviewers. You'll also find a long list of places to go on your bike and many bike-related links.

Triathlete Online
http://www.EmporiumOne.COM/Triathlete/
Triathlete-letters@TriathleteMag.COM

Like most online magazines, Triathlete Online includes top headlines right on the first page, with a graphical index to the major departments: What's New (news bulletins), Race Results, Calendar, Forum, Next Month, Photo Gallery, TriMart, and Back Issues (full text of features and columns). The Forum section offers readers the opportunity to interact with writers, editors, and each other, discussing such issues as drafting, race day preparation routines, training tips, getting started, and comments on specific events. Some of the articles include a contents list at the start so that in a review of running shoes, for example, you can jump to the brand you want to read about or scroll through the entire document. You can also search the top menus (but not individual documents—although you may be able to by now) throughout the site for specific topics and, of course, subscribe to the print version. Specific columns address the art and science of cycling as well as duathlon. Chuck Rucker serves as the online editor for this excellent triathlon resource.

Triathlete Online brings you the best in news, advice, and race coverage.

VeloNews
http://www.velonews.com/VeloNews/
VeloWWW@AOL.com

One of the biggest names in cycling periodicals has gone online and done it right (thanks to Chris Rice, Tim Johnson, and Chas Chamberlin). Frequent visitors will appreciate the This Just In section of late-breaking news. Major events, ranging from the Interbike show to the Tour de France, have their own pages and are listed in the text index on the main page. The Contents section includes several full-text articles and news from the current issue plus a complete table of contents. You can check VeloNews' calendar for races and other cycling events and browse through Velo Merchandise and reader Classifieds (or check the VeloSwap area in season). Patrick O'Grady has his entertaining cartoons online here, and if you're tired of plain cycling, you can jump to Inside Triathlon. As you would expect, VeloNews offers a nice, well-organized collection of cycling-related links from which to choose. You can also request a free issue and learn more about the VeloNews online effort.

Winning Magazine
http://www.winningmag.com/index.html
winning@WinningMag.com

Winning Magazine Online is yet another cycling periodical that takes advantage of the Internet's timeliness and multimedia features. You first see headlines for (and links to) the most current stories in road and mountain bike racing. Winning covers major races, such as the Tour de France and the Olympics, and offers a Marketplace, Gallery Forum, photographs, top cycling stories, and upcoming events plus searchable archives from back issues (starting with July 1995). In fact, the entire site can be searched for items of interest. As with other online magazines, you can subscribe to the printed version using an online form (or call toll-free). When you're done browsing Winning, you can jump to Triathlete Online or to the Gatorade Cooler Site (multisport coverage) or send editor Chuck Rucker your thoughts via e-mail.

Winning Magazine Online is the place to for racing news, results, and photos.

Chapter 10

Nutrition, Sports Medicine, and Training

You'll find lots of online help for your training efforts, whether in preparation for a century, a cross-country race, a criterium, or a tour. The quality of this advice varies widely. Be sure to check on the credentials of anyone offering nutrition or medical suggestions—a polite request should be acceptable to anyone who sincerely wants to help you get a competitive edge *safely*. As with any claim, if it sounds too good to be true, it probably is. You can read Chapter 14 for more recommendations on deciding how to use online advice. This chapter reviews sites that provide nutrition, sports medicine, and training information as well as other aids, such as software (check Jørn Dahl-Stamnes' Velocipede in Chapter 4, too). You'll find plenty of training advice on the sci.med.nutrition and misc.fitness newsgroups and on the coaching mailing list (at VeloNet). Much more training software is available, as you'll discover once you're online (see Appendix E as well).

Ask the Coach Column/On-Line Training Manual for Vets
http://econ-www.newcastle.edu.au/~bill/q&a.html

As part of his WWW Sports Page, Bill Mitchell offers dozens of cycling links plus some local features, such as his Ask the Coach Column and On-Line Training Manual for Vets. Ask the Coach topics include weekly training patterns, overtraining, ergometer bike work, and intervals and recovery. You can e-mail your questions to Ask the Coach (ecwfm@cc.newcastle.edu.au) or ask while you're at the page. His On-Line Training Manual for Veteran Riders is a compilation of his work with the Hunter Academy of Cycling head coach to design a scientifically based training program for the "40-year-old rider who works full-time and has other commitments...[and] who wants to go hard still." Bill's efforts will eventually be published as a book, but you can take advantage of his progress with the excellent online guide, which is well written and documented. Be sure to thank him when you visit.

The Athlete's Diary
http://alumni.caltech.edu/~slp/tad.html

Steve Patt's The Athlete's Diary is a popular multisport training log available for Windows, Macintosh, and DOS. At Steve's Web site, you can read the complete list of features (very long and comprehensive), excerpts from published reviews, unsolicited testimonials from users, and ordering information. You can also download a demo copy for any of the operating systems noted above; the demo software is full-featured but is limited to 25 entries (if you purchase an unrestricted copy, you don't need to start over).

Chiropractic
http://gcn.scri.fsu.edu/~dunnet/

Dr. John Dunn welcomes you to the "Wonderful World of Chiropractic," where he offers a few self-help tips to prevent pain caused by athletic strain and injuries. These short documents briefly describe the type and source of pain addressed by the tip and then give suggestions that you can do at home. You'll also be able to learn all you need to know about Dr. Dunn himself and his practice and can send him questions or comments.

Endurance Training Journal
http://s2.com:80/etj/

The Endurance Training Journal is "The Journal of the Monomaniacal Endurance Athlete" but is especially friendly to cyclists. This site isn't like other online magazines since it is not updated regularly and keeps the core set of articles available at all times. The Training section is divided among topics related to cycling, running, swimming, triathlon, and women in sports. In addition to several articles specific to cycling, you'll find information about periodization of training (off-season, in season, active rest), lactic acid, lactate threshold, massage, overtraining, leg length, tempo training, oral contraceptives and endurance training, and how to train with a heart rate monitor. Tips for training in hot, cold, and high-altitude environments are available too, as are several nutrition-related pieces. The multisport coverage and sports medicine clinic will help you develop effective cross-training programs and stay healthy and injury-free throughout the season. Jeff Rogers, who operates the ETJ, has posted articles by such respected experts as Edmund Burke, PhD (who also serves as managing editor).

> *I live on the east coast of Australia north of Sydney and have raced extensively throughout the world as an amateur cyclist. I also teach in a university and have become interested in what happens to top-level bike racers as they get older, a subject close to my heart. Most of the cycle training literature is aimed at the recreational and/or young racing cyclist. I have attempted to bridge that gap by designing a dedicated training plan for the veteran cyclist who still wishes to go race hard but has less time and requires longer recovery. I provide a guide for structuring a quality program, which individuals can tailor to their own specific constraints. I also provide advice via e-mail, and my pages provide the best results and news service in the southern hemisphere.*
>
> Bill Mitchell, Ask the Coach/On-Line Training Manual for Vets

Exercise Log

http://fas-www.harvard.edu/~maurits/ExerciseLog.html

Maurits van der Veen has written a Hypercard-based (i.e., Macintosh) activities log that allows you to track your workouts for just about any sport. You can read a detailed description of the software's features, which include entry fields for date, sport, workout type, distance, pace, pulse, weather, and much more. The program also has import/export capabilities, shortcuts built in to eliminate repetitive entries, and an extensive help section. Maurits includes links to sites where you can download the software, or you can send e-mail (maurits@fas.harvard.edu) requesting a copy. Don't forget to send him a check to cover the extremely reasonable shareware cost.

The Endurance Training Journal offers many excellent articles for cyclists at all levels of competition.

http de Charles: The Internet's Fitness Resource
http://rampages.onramp.net/~chaz/

Charles Rotblut is an ACE-certified personal trainer who has combined his
fitness knowledge with his Web page–building skills to produce as complete a
list of Internet fitness sites as possible. In addition to a handful of top-notch
cycling links, you'll learn about fitness organizations online. Diet, Nutrition,
and Weight Loss resources include documents, software, and links such as the
USDA nutrient database. He includes separate sections for FAQs (abdominal
muscle training, misc.fitness, rec.bicycles, stretching, triathlon, etc.), newsgroups, fitness magazines, and academic sites. The academic sites in particular will help anyone looking for sound scientific information. Among the
FAQs is a link to the ACL Page (anterior cruciate ligament), where you'll find
information on injuries to this structure. You'll be able to use his links to
running, weight lifting, aerobics, and inline skating sites when you're ready to
start your cross-training program.

International Food Information Council
http://ificinfo.health.org/

The International Food Information Council provides nutrition and food-
related information for health care professionals, educators, parents, consum-
ers, and journalists. You can easily navigate the entire site thanks to well-
organized indices and cross references. Online brochures and newsletters
cover several age groups, special needs, and food topics (including nutrition
quackery), and FAQs are available for caffeine, *E. coli*, and monosodium
glutamate (MSG). You can try the link to the Food and Drug Administration
for more information on food-related topics.

The Medical Tent
http://riceinfo.rice.edu:80/~jenkins/

Mark Jenkins, MD has created a home page that any cyclist or endurance
athlete will probably want to visit at some point. Material is available on
stretching, the heart and heart rate monitors, hydration and fluid balance,
and a long list of individual subjects, such as overtraining, ergogenic aids,
and high-altitude training. The information available here is pooled from
published medical sources, scientific research, discussions on the
rec.sport.triathlon newsgroup (Dr. Jenkins frequently contributes valuable
information to newsgroup threads as well), and real-life patient situations.
You can be sure the recommendations here are safe and scientifically sound.
In addition to entering The Medical Tent, you can look over the Rice
University Cycling Team and photographs from races around the world.

Neuromuscular Physiology
http://ortho84-13.ucsd.edu/MusIntro/Jump.html

The Neuromuscular Physiology Laboratory at the University of California, San Diego, has as part of its department Web site a nice tutorial on the "basic science of muscle." Topics include fat metabolism, glucose metabolism, cellular energy stores, muscle-joint interactions, muscle fiber types, eccentric contraction, and much more. The documents are well written and are cross-referenced with hypertext links. The graphics are useful and should be available as postscript files if you only have a text browser. Be sure to thank Tom Burkholder for maintaining the site so well.

Nutrition Guide
http://128.196.106.42/nutrition.html

The Arizona Health Sciences Library maintains a comprehensive online guide to nutrition resources for every level of user. The Guide organizes nutrition topics by subject, format, and index. The Guide hasn't been updated in some time but includes links to major indices and search engines as well as academic centers with nutrition databases or centers online. If you want to track down some information that goes beyond the usual quick tips, try here for some starting points.

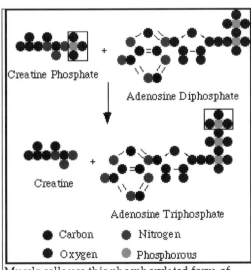

Muscle cells use this phosphorylated form of creatine to store energy. Normal metabolism can not produce energy as quickly as a muscle cell can use it, so an extra storage source is needed. The phosphate group can be quickly transferred to ADP to regenerate the ATP necessary for muscle contraction. Hydrolysis of creatine phosphate to creatine releases 10.3 kcal/mole.

Anyone interested in learning the nitty-gritty details with regard to how muscles work and which sources of energy are used by cells during exercise will appreciate the University of California, San Diego Neuromuscular Physiology Lab Web site.

The Nutrition Pages
http://deja-vu.oldiron.cornell.edu/~jabbo/

Tim Triche, Jr., contributes to sci.med.nutrition and wrote some of the sports nutrition portion of the FAQ (which he includes on his Nutrition Pages). His graphical display of nutrition links and information will help just about anyone looking for advice on what to eat, and his essays on nutrition topics are thought-provoking. You'll be linked to nutrition and fitness newsgroups, gopher servers, and Web sites at various places on these pages.

Pro Trainer
http://www.indy.net/~pauld/HomePage.html

Paul Filliman, PE has written Pro Trainer Sports Training Software, a multisport workout log and training planner. You can use the program to schedule and then later to analyze your workouts to optimize your training and reach your goals. Pro Trainer supports multiple bikes and routes, off-season cross-training, custom training plans, and much more. Paul offers you a Hypercard tour of the software, a save-locked version of the software (requires Bin Hex, HQXer, or Stuffit Expander), and a short set of cycling, running, and triathlon links. He also lists the current (and reasonable) cost of requesting the full program with documentation and custom add-ons.

Sports and Exercise Psychology
http://spot.colorado.edu/~collinsj/

Julia Collins has listed on the Web professional sports organizations and societies that take an interest in sports psychology and sociology. Contact, journal, and conference information is included for the Association for the Advancement of Applied Sport Psychology, the North American Society for the Psychology of Sport and Physical Activity, WomenSport International, the American Psychological Association, and the American College of Sports Medicine (among others). Sports-related conferences and graduate programs in applied sports psychology are also announced here.

Stretching FAQ
http://archie.ac.il/papers/rma/stretching_1.html
http://www.cis.ohio-state.edu/hypertext/faq/usenet/stretching/top.html

Bradford Appleton has been improving the Stretching FAQ since he first undertook the project in 1993. Just about every aspect of stretching is covered: physiology, flexibility, types of stretching, how to stretch, working toward the splits, and normal ranges of joint motion. You'll also find a list of references on stretching and an index to the entire document, which is available on the Web with hypertext links or as a text file (in several formats).

Training-Nutrition Home Page
http://www.dgsys.com/~trnutr/index.html

Paul Moses operates the training-nutrition mailing list (send `subscribe` in the *subject* line to trnutreq@dgs.dgsys.com) and its corresponding home page mainly as a service to body builders and athletes who are concerned about nutrition and weight training. You should read the FAQ to learn more about the list, and you can read the list archives to get an idea of the type of information exchanged. Paul has pulled out some useful documents (such as a glycemic index and seafood nutrient information) at the top of his page. His links run from biochemical explanations of nutrition to weight lifting.

Vegetarian Pages
http://www.veg.org/veg/

The Vegetarian Pages, maintained by Geraint "Gedge" Edwards, are updated regularly and include a list of new items added to the site and a current schedule of vegetarian events around the world. This site has the World Guide to Vegetarianism (a hypertext list of restaurants, organizations, and other regional vegetarian information from around the world), the Vegetarian Society of the United Kingdom (not just for Britons), the Vegetarian Resource Group, and Veggies Unite! (online searchable vegetarian cookbook). You'll find FAQs from rec.food.veg and the VEGAN-L mailing list, multilingual phrases for traveling vegetarians, glossaries and dictionaries, reading materials, Vegetarian News, and the Mega Index to Vegetarian Information. Books, software, organizations, recipes, famous vegetarians, and online vegetarians are all discussed here.

Spiders in the Web

Flashy Web sites filled with misinformation are looking for your gold card. Cyberspace predators peddling potions, herbs, and "cures" are hungry. No longer do they have to seek you out. They just lie and wait for you to come to them. Spiders in dark corners. Determined to find the answer to the fatigue that has been plaguing your rides, you flip on your computer and jack into the Net. Pictures of smiling professional athletes—juxtaposed with bold text and mesmerizing graphics—hyping the virtues of the latest magic energy bar, creep onto your screen. Snared, you reach for your credit card. The encoded numbers flash from your screen into the ether, and the spider gets a little fatter.

Spiders in the Web

Mark A. Jenkins, MD, NCAA Team Physician

Yahoo Nutrition Resources
http://www.yahoo.com/Health/Nutrition/

You'll say Yahoo! when you use any of the sections provided by this enterprising company. Yahoo! Corporation (also described in Chapter 12) provides brief descriptions and links to thousands of Internet sites, including hundreds of interest to cyclists. The nutrition section includes commercial, academic, and consumer sites that will meet just about anyone's needs. If you don't see what you want, Yahoo! will help you search the Internet to track down that specific item.

Zero Fat
http://www.zerofat.com

If you've ever wanted to learn everything you possibly can about cutting the fat out of your diet, you need to visit the Zero Fat page. Actually, you'll learn a lot more than just how to reduce your fat intake. The folks at Purgative Productions share the latest information on nutrition, exercise, supplements, fat-burning drugs, and psychology. Facts about fats abound, as do links to FAQs and nutrition Web sites and Usenet newsgroups.

You'll be overjoyed to use Yahoo to find nutrition and other cycling resources.

Each of us is engaged in a quest to make the most of our personal allotment of talent. The online interaction with others of varying experience and expertise offers perspective: clues and shortcuts to the effortless grace and efficiency we revere in elite cyclists. Skill is a matter of principles, or "tricks," if you will, and as a coach, I search for every way to light up the light bulbs in my students, to find that particular expression which renders a concept useful. The challenge of communicating these principles across cyberspace brings the tremendous reward of having encouraged and guided riders from all corners of the globe, knowing that in some way I have helped spur them on to the highest possible level of personal elegance in whatever sort of cycling they pursue.

Ginny Wilken, USCF Expert Coaching license, District 5 Coach

Chapter 11

Triathlon and Duathlon

Triathletes and duathletes have benefited from the explosion of cycling resources and have brought their own sport online in force. The sites described in this chapter are the major meccas of multisport and will lead you to just about every triathlon Web page available. Many regional triathlon pages provide local race schedules and results as well as links to local resources (Chapter 13). Once you're online, you'll find several triathlon-related user home pages that aren't listed here but are worthy of a visit.

Amalgamated Calendar
http://www.webcom.com/~rooworld/amalgamated_calendar.html

A small detour in RooWorld (as in, Quintana Roo), the Amalgamated Calendar is a one-stop shopping trip for multisport race calendars, including triathlon, cycling, running, and swimming. Use this site if you're looking for race information and don't want to wade through pages of results and training tips on the way. Of course, you might get distracted by the links back to RooWorld, its technical library, and its massive list of sites.

Dead Runners Society Triathlete's Home Page
http://www.cris.com/~thompete/tri-drs/tridrs.shtml

The Dead Runners Society, one of the most active mailing lists online, maintains its own Triathlete's Home Page to allow "Dead Runners who would like to talk about training for and racing in multisport events a facility to do so." You'll find instructions for joining the Society's triathlete subgroup (`subscribe tri-drs your name` to listserv@listserv.dartmouth.edu), an introduction to the group, and archives from the list (mainly training tips). Available links take you to other triathlon and running sites.

MultiSport Online
http://multisport.com/mol/

MultiSport Online is the service "built by athletes, for athletes." The free basic membership allows you to check on upcoming events and includes a listing in the Multisport White Pages. You'll be able to access anything from the main menu: results, prerace registration, chat forums, and information about weather conditions and travel suggestions. The premium service includes news feeds, custom e-mail addresses, and directory services for athletes, clubs, and teams. Race directors and coordinators can use their own private area to get help planning and managing their event.

Osmar's Sport's Page
http://fas.sfu.ca/cs/people/GradStudents/zaiane/personal/sports.html

Osmar Rachid Zaiane has a home page with dozens of triathlon, swimming, biking, running, and rock climbing links from which to choose. You won't find training information or racing tips locally, but all the best sites are listed in this one convenient site. Osmar's site is good for locating regional triathlon links and keeping up with new sites as they come online.

PB's Triathlon Home Page
http://www.vicnet.net.au/~ironman/tri/tri.htm

Many triathletes have their own home pages, but PB's (Paul Wilson) is a must see. In the section for Australia, you can check on results, upcoming races (triathlon, duathlon, and ironman), and triathlon organizations down under. The same sort of information for races around the world is available on the International page. In the training section, you'll find the Triathlon FAQ, articles on swimming, and a link to the Endurance Training Journal. You can also scroll through Paul's list of tri-related Usenet newsgroups and Web sites, which includes a brief description of what you'll find.

RST Magazine
http://www.webcom.com/~sp/brug/rst.html

Pat Brug points out that RST could stand for many things, but in this case, it represents the rec.sport.triathlon team (like Team Internet for rec.bicycles). You can learn about the team's doings here and how to order team clothing (through RooWorld). As Team RST becomes more organized, this site will no doubt expand to fill the role played by any organized racing club.

Paul Wilson's Triathlon Home Page covers the sport all around the globe.

Please let me know who reads these pages and what you want to see. Complete PB's Survey.

AUSTRALIAN TRIATHLON SCENE

My Australian Triathlon Page has all the latest news, results and calendars from Down Under.
Includes Entry Form for Australian Duathlon Championships, Canberra, 27 Aug.

TRIATHLONS ABROAD

The International Triathlon Page contains all the overseas results, news and gossip.
Here you will find ITU World Cup results and other Major International results.

IRONMAN TRIATHLONS

Ironman Triathlons are so special that they deserve a page of their own! [Very much under construction.]

 ALL YOU NEED IS NEWS

Find out what is happening all around the globe, ask questions, meet new friends and generally keep up to date. It's all here in the various Usenet newsgroups. Of interest to the triathlete are:

Running and Triathlon
http://canyon.epg.harris.com/~mvm/runtri.html

Matt Mahoney emphasizes running (including ultrarunning) on his triathlon page, but you'll find some interesting articles available only here. His links include several triathlon and running sites plus a list of general outdoor recreation links, such as Utah's National Parks and the Great Outdoor Recreation Pages (GORP).

Triathlete's Web
http://w3.one.net/~triweb/triweb.html

Marty Miller has outdone himself bringing the Triathlete's Web to the world. You'll find the Triathlon and Ironman Canada FAQs, schedules and results of races from all over the world, the Tri-Fed Competitive Rules, triathlon magazines, and much more. Hints for Safe Cycling by Rolf "Ironman" Arands lists a number of common sense safety tips (compiled from rec.sport.triathlon) to use during training rides. Marty has several lists of links organized according to whether they are triathlon, commercial, swimming, cycling, running, newsgroups, nutrition (lots of beer sites), and a collection of his favorite non-tri spots on the Web. New items are conveniently flagged as such, and the index at the top of the page will take you straight to the area of most interest.

The Ironman triathlon—an event for the extraordinary person, the person with the best genetics, and the person with natural athletic ability. Not. I am an ordinary guy with ordinary genes who has done this extraordinary event twice. The preparation for an Ironman is intense but not insurmountable. Taken in pieces, the Ironman is very doable ... extraordinarily difficult, but given good preparation, it can be done. Preparation, all of the stuff that comes with doing the event, is one of the keys to success. Logistics such as race entry, traveling, accommodations, and the more subtle mental preparation all require information. A balance between physical and mental rest from training is necessary. In fact, less training is better if the goals are set carefully. This comes with experience. I am still learning. Fortunately, the Internet is a vast resource for information and shared experience, with athletes from all over the world accessible on your desktop. While the Ironman may not be for everyone, I hope few people say to themselves "I cannot do that because I am not good enough." It can be done by mere mortals. The victory in the Ironman is in the struggle. To toe the line is the first victory. To finish is the icing on the cake.

Rolf Arands, arands@sol.rutgers.edu, Ironman Canada (1994, 1995)

Triathlon!
http://www.ens-lyon.fr/~desprez/FILES/TRIATH/triath.html

Frédéric Desprez has set up a terrific triathlon page from his home in Bordeaux, France. In addition to providing a solid set of tri-links, he lets you in on his swimming workouts, offers you training log software, lists all triathlons and duathlons to be held in France, and shows you his own racing schedule and results. Frédéric also includes pictures and a place to e-mail him comments and additions.

Triathlon & Cycling Home Page
http://dragon.acadiau.ca/~005963m/jay_homepage.html

Jason MacDonald's home page is dedicated to triathlon with a special emphasis on cycling. The main menu is a streamlined set of choices designed for graphical browsers. You can check one page for training and racing information, another with links to commercial sites supporting triathlon sports, another describing newsgroups (including links if your browser supports Usenet), another with local race schedules (Nova Scotia and Canada), and another with Web links organized by sport (triathlon, running, cycling, swimming). New additions are highlighted on their own page, so frequent visitors don't need to check through each directory individually whenever they visit. Jason's home page index includes triathlon, personal, and local (Truro, Nova Scotia) links. Canadian triathletes and duathletes will appreciate his schedule of races, which covers eastern Canada in particular.

Triathletes in Canada and throughout the world will appreciate Jason MacDonald's Triathlon & Cycling Home Page.

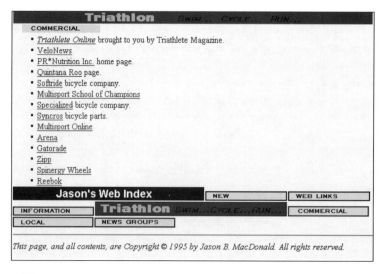

Chapter 12

Catalogs, Indices, and Search Engines

If you want to find just about anything about any aspect of cycling, you should be able to do so with relative ease. Several intrepid cybercyclists have established pages upon pages of links to virtually every known cycling resource in the world. You can skim through any of the sites listed in this chapter to see which index best meets your needs and interests. Some are better organized than others, some are updated more frequently and include reviews of individual sites (it's nice to know what to expect before transferring). You can also use one of many Internet search engines to look up individual cycling topics by keyword. These search engines are easy to use and, especially during off-hours (evening, weekend), are quite fast. You can think of them as automated card catalogs for the Internet.

Bicycling Information
http://www.cs.unc.edu/~barman/bicycle.html

Dilip Barman has a Web page with an assortment of Web links plus a handy list of e-mail addresses for companies, magazines, organizations, and individuals. Other sites are much more comprehensive, but Dilip offers some unique sites and flags new sites as they come online.

The Big Ring
http://nsns.com/BigRing/

The Big Ring page of links, maintained by Charlie Hofacker, includes WWW, gopher, Usenet newsgroup, and mailing list options covering a variety of topics, such as women, mountain biking, racing, and tandems. You'll also find links to some of the best index sites reviewed elsewhere in this chapter and to a few online magazines. The Big Ring is still growing and is a fast, manageable place to look for important online cycling resources.

The Big Ring puts you in high gear in your search for cycling information.

The *Big Ring* is a page of hyperlinks pointing to biking activity on the net. If you know of any pedaling-related resources, drop us a line using the email address at the bottom of the page. And if you are interested in peddling-related resources, click on our button at the bottom of the page.

BikIndex
http://www.voicenet.com/~mudboy

Pete Ruckelshaus maintains his labor of love, the BikIndex, as a Web document (formerly a Usenet posting until it grew too large). This index of bicycle manufacturers includes just about every company that is in some way involved with cycling (including multisport), as well as professional teams and "Bike Industry Movers and Shakers." You'll find frame builders, component manufacturers, clothing companies, nutritional products, software, publications, retailers, travel and tour companies, and "stuff that doesn't quite fit elsewhere. ..." Pete divides the list into Web URLs and e-mail addresses so that anyone with a computer and a modem can reach these people.

The Cycle Center: The Big Index
http://www.mindspring.com/~roadkill/cycles/index.html

Tim Stewart maintains The Cycle Center, an organized index to cycling sites throughout the Internet. You'll find a handy table of contents at the top that will take you straight to individual topics throughout his page. Most areas have self-explanatory names, such as Bicycle Commuting and Organizations and Clubs. Cool Links is a sort of "best of" group of sites, ranging from unique groups, such as WOMBATS and C.H.U.N.K. 666, to good all-around spots, such as VeloNet and Mountain Biking. Tim includes a few words describing the site and organizes them by general category. He has links not found elsewhere, but this isn't an exhaustive listing (which makes it easier to peruse).

Junior Web spinner Tim Stewart offers a central site for cycling resources.

I started my BIKINDEX for two reasons: one to combine my two main hobbies, bikes and computers; and the other as a purely selfish attempt to feed my addiction to information and connectivity. The more people who knew about BIKINDEX, the more people could provide me with new URLs and e-mail addresses. Also, because I am teaching myself HTML, this is the place where I can try out all of my new efforts and ideas.
Pete Ruckelshaus

Cycling the InfoBahn
http://www.veloworks.com/cycling.html

Bikiebob has created Cycling the InfoBahn to complement his tremendous online activity. (Bikiebob is a fountain of advice, opinions, and technical information for the online cycling community, as are many of the people who maintain pages discussed in this chapter and throughout the book.) He starts his page off with the current year race results (men and women), rankings, and team rosters; further down you'll find links to online magazines that cover racing (such as VeloNews, Cycling Plus, and Winning) and to sites that will help you train for your own competitive efforts. He also has a link to Team Internet. Newspapers on the InfoBahn include the San Jose Mercury-News, the San Francisco Chronicle & Examiner, and the Daily Telegraph of London. He also invites RetroGrouches to unite at Rivendell Bicycle Works (http://www.best.com/~bikiebob/rivendell/index.html) and Bridgestone Owners to come together on the Internet BOB (Bridgestone Owners Bunch) mailing list (internet-bob-request@netcom.com). By the way, the name on Bikiebob's birth certificate should read something like Steven Sheffield.

The Internet, as part of the highly touted Information Superhighway, has many uses, yet the mass media tends to only focus on the educational and commercial aspects. However, I, along with many other cyclists, have found the Internet an extension of the community of cyclists.

Cycling is one of the fastest-growing sports in the United States yet is still essentially ignored by the commercial media. The Internet has provided a forum for cyclists to connect with others who share the same interest. Cyclists in Europe keep their North American counterparts apprised of results of races on both the professional and amateur circuits, often in extreme detail, while local sources only print a short squib and a list of top-10 finishers (if any attention is paid at all).

Where else can one get advice on racing tactics from current and former professional cyclists? Have problems understanding how to true a wheel? Ask the man who wrote the book (Jobst Brandt, jbrandt@hpl.hp.com). Got a question about Campagnolo components? Ask the factory representative (Jeff Kratka, jkratka@aol.com). Have questions about a particular brand of bicycle? Ask the community at large, sit back, and watch the opinions roll by.

Flames abound, but so does an incredible amount of valuable information. All you need to do is hop on the electronic paceline.

Steven L. Sheffield

Cycling Related Pages
http://www.cis.upenn.edu/~vinson/cycling.html

Jack Vinson has organized a great collection of cycling Web sites that cover racing (results and teams), regional information (especially Philadelphia but the rest of the world too), online magazines, commercial sites, cycling organizations, individual user home pages, and tandems. As with most well-organized lists of links, Jack includes an index at the top to allow you to jump to the area of most interest. At the very top, you'll find a link to the venerable U.S. Bicycle Hall of Fame (see Chapter 4).

Galaxy
http://galaxy.einet.net/galaxy/Leisure-and-Recreation/Sports/Biking.html

TradeWave (formerly EINet) offers its Galaxy guide to the Internet as a public service, and it's quite a service. New items are flagged at the top, and the entire Biking guide is arranged according to the resource provided (guides, collections, events, etc.). You can search the whole Galaxy and add new URLs to make it more complete. As more cyclists stop by and leave their calling cards, Galaxy will become more useful. However, several user-created index pages, such as Steve Ciccarelli's, and some other commercial catalogs, such as Yahoo, have many more links available.

Lycos, Inc.: The Catalog of the Internet
http://www.lycos.com/

Lycos is a comprehensive catalog of the Internet that is updated daily. You can use the Lycos search form to locate information about cycling topics (and anything else you might need to research) in its databases. The big catalog has almost 8 million Web pages—no doubt more by now—or about 98% of the content of the WWW. You'll be given a list of possible matches arranged in descending order of relevance. Lycos includes the URL, the authors, a description, and an abstract of each site (sample return shown below).

---

1) Cycling Related Pages On Www [1.0000, 2 of 2 terms, adj 0.9]

Outline: Cycling Related Pages On Www Index Bicycle Race Results WWW Links To Area-Specific **Cycling** Information WWW Links To Area-Specific **Cycling** Information **Cycling** Businesses and Organizations on the Net Magazines

Abstract: Cycling Related Pages On Www Last Update 19 July 1995 Bicycle Hall of Fame Index * Race Results * **Cycling** Teams * Regional **Cycling** Info, especially Philadelphia * **Cycling** oriented businesses and organizations * **Cycling** related magazines * Interesting **cycling** info * Bike People with **cycling** pages * Tandem Enthusiasts Bicycle Race Results * 1995 Giro d'Italia * Another Giro d'Italia page by IBM (sponsor of the race) * Colorado Mountain Bike Racing * WWW Links To Area-Specific **Cycling** Information
http://www.cis.upenn.edu/~vinson/cycling.html (16k)

[Home | Search | Lists | Reference | Add/Delete | News | Lycos Inc]

In addition to its straightforward search form, the Lycos, Inc. catalog offers a unique and valuable service: you can preview what's available at each of the sites that comes back from your search.

Steve C's Bicycling Page (now The Cyberrider Cycling WWW Site)
http://blueridge.infomkt.ibm.com/bikes/

Steve Ciccarelli has created one of the great cycling meccas on the Internet. Although it caters to touring, tandem, and ultra riders (the UltraMarathon Cycling Association is headquartered here), this site has "all manner of cycling-related links," and archives of all the rec.bicycles newsgroups. Two of Steve's great features are an alphabetical index to all the hundreds of links included on his pages, and full-text searching of his Web site. Several local sites (to the Washington, DC, area) and national organizations (such as the League of American Bicyclists) are conveniently included at the top, followed by directories full of useful information and links: Tandems; Ride Writeups (from rec.bicycles.rides); Rider Info & Advice (long rides & touring); Events; Places; News (Usenet newsgroups); Cue Sheets (for local rides); Equipment (nice collection of articles); Info Sources & Advocacy; Bike Yukon, Fiction & Humor (including Spike Bike); Pictures; and Raw info (includes the entire biking subdirectory structure). He concludes his main cycling page with a list of "neat" sites, such as Cool Site of the Day, the UIUC Weather Machine, the Virtual Reference Desk, and several other interesting spots on the Web.

The Internet has been a great help to me in my fledgling cycling career. In late 1993, I resolved to take up cycle commuting as a means of getting back into shape, although I hadn't been on a bike in almost 10 years. Through a Washington DC area e-mail list, DCBIKE, I began conversing with John Boone, with whom I began doing local club rides. John arranged for a good-quality loaner bike to get me started. Soon, I was strong enough to occasionally ride the 34-mile round trip to work.

Early in 1994, my job began requiring frequent trips to the Silicon Valley area. As an addicted cyclist and Internet user, I looked to the Net to try to arrange some way of cycling during my business trips. I posted to rec.bicycles.rides asking about organized rides around Palo Alto. A week later, I found myself on a rickety rented Raleigh 10-speed, wheel to wheel (but not for long!) with three RAAM riders on a 24-hour training ride. On that day, I learned more about distance riding than I ever thought possible. Within a week or two, I had broken my previous best distance, and six weeks later, I completed a 300K event. By the end of that summer, I was able to hold my own on a 120-mile ride with some of those same riders.

My own Web site started as a set of documents that I had saved for information and inspiration, but it soon grew beyond that. It's my own small effort to help others enjoy the many facets of cycling.

Steve Ciccarelli

Virtual Breakaway
http://www.eskimo.com/~cycling/breakaway.html

Brent Soderberg has made the Virtual Breakaway (formerly Cycling the Net) as straightforward and easy to use as possible (see the shot of his site in Chapter 3). He includes useful links when describing certain resources, such as those to FTP sites that archive newsgroup messages, and he includes short instructions to help you on your way when necessary. The Road Racing and Results section is further divided into the Tour de France, International and Pro Racing, Cycling Teams, Other Racing Information, and Racing Images. Most sites are self-explanatory, and Brent adds a few words to help you understand those that aren't. If you like this site, don't miss Brent's Virtual Peleton (http://www.eskimo.com/~cycling/index.html).

Virtual Library
http://www.atm.ch.cam.ac.uk/sports/wheel.html

Owen Garrett, chief librarian at the Virtual Library, keeps a number of cycling-related pages on the shelves. Links are given a brief description if they aren't self-explanatory. This isn't a comprehensive site, but it should be up-to-date and have a good selection to satisfy the needs and interests of just about anyone who rides.

WebCrawler
http://webcrawler.com/

WebCrawler maintains an indexed database of all the material (text, graphics, titles, etc.) available on the WWW. You search this database by keyword and receive a list of possible links ranked according to how well each returned "hit" matches your request (no description, though). WebCrawler is surprisingly fast and almost never comes up empty, so be sure to try it when you need to hunt down a specialized topic on the Internet.

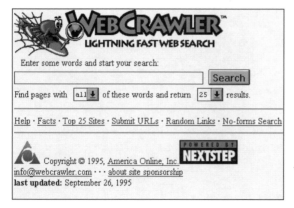

WebCrawler is one of the fastest, easiest ways to track down cycling information on the Internet.

Whole Internet Catalog

http://nearnet.gnn.com/gnn/wic/rec.toc.html
http://gnn.com/gnn/meta/sports/other/cycling.html

The Whole Internet Catalog, by Global Network Navigator from O'Reilly & Associates, provides links for sports and fitness topics and health-related categories (among hundreds of others). Despite its name, the Whole Internet Catalog is not as comprehensive as Yahoo and other Internet catalogs. However, rather than just being dumped at the site listed, you will be taken to a short paragraph about it; from there you can go to the resource or return to the index. You can also check the cycling page on GNN Sports, though the list of links there is not particularly impressive.

WWW Bicycle Lane

http://www.cs.purdue.edu/homes/dole/bike.html

Bryn Dole has maintained the WWW Bicycle Lane for some time now and has done an outstanding job at that (his page received three chili peppers from the WWW Cycling Links). The table of contents at the top of the page lets you head straight to the topic of your choice, depending on what information you need. Be sure to check what's currently in his Cool Links list, which he updates with the latest links worth visiting (such as "Project Chopper—Finnish bad boys and their bikes" and "Chain Reaction—Bringing people together through art" … on a bike trip). In addition to scores of Web links, Bryn offers online forms, gopher servers, FTP sites, photographs, and mailing list information. You'll also appreciate the brief descriptions of sites that aren't self-explanatory. You can ride the Bicycle Lane with either a text or graphical browser, but you might have to wait a minute or two for it to load over a slow connection (the site is huge!).

You can rely on Bryn Dole to keep his catalog of Internet cycling resources current.

The WWW Bicycle Lane

© Copyright Bryn Dole, 1995.

Table of Contents:
WWW: Cool Links | Bicycle Commuting | Magazines | Lists of Sites | Companies | Organizations and Clubs | Rides and Touring Information | Racing Calendars and Information | Mountain Biking | Bicycle Safety | USCF Teams on the Internet
Other Resources: Online Forms | Gopher Sites | FTP sites | Biking Pictures | Mailing Lists

WWW Cycling Links

http://psy.ucsd.edu/~mtaffe/CycleLink.html

Ken Manning and Mike Taffe maintain a terrific list of WWW links "as a service to r.b.r. [rec.bicycles.racing]." They even offer a rating system with red and green chili peppers, updating their chili awards as the sites themselves are updated and improved. You start off with the Top Spots and move along through a well-organized list (with table of contents links at the top of the page) that concludes with Cycling's Best and Worst. Much of the page is devoted to road sites, but you'll find all the usual suspects. One unique feature is Ken's Big Wall Cycling Stock Index, which is updated weekly with stock prices and includes a chart of the Index's progress, cycling industry news (and commentary), and corporate links.

Yahoo Cycling Resources

http://www.yahoo.com/Recreation/Sports/Cycling/
http://www.yahoo.com/Business_and_Economy/Products_and_Services/Magazines/Sports/Cycling/

This aptly named subject-oriented catalog for the Internet is a great place to check for links to every imaginable topic, including cycling. Major categories have additional lists of resources nested within them so that no one directory is too overwhelming (see the figure of Yahoo's main Nutrition section in Chapter 10 to see how pages are organized). You can search the entire Yahoo! Corporation catalog itself as well. Yahoo describes some resources in addition to providing a direct link. Yahoo has its own powerful Web-searching tools and links to other search engines, such as WebCrawler, Lycos, EINet Galaxy, Aliweb, and CUSI Search Engines. Yahoo is updated regularly, so keep a place on your hot list for this hot site on the Web.

On the WWW Cycling Links, more chili peppers means a hotter site.

Top Spots *to get you started...*

Bicycling Hall of Fame

♪♪♪ If you don't stop here, you can't call yourself a cyclist.

Roger Marquis' HomePage

♪♪♪ If you don't know who Roger is then your USCF license number has 6 figures. There is a lot of great racing info here, very few graphics, though. There is one great photo, but Roger misspelled "Prehn".

International Human Powered Vehicle Association (IHPVA)

♪♪♪ Lots of great photos and info on anything powered by humans alone.

Decavitator

♪♪♪ This page has great style and unique information about a unique side of pedal-powered activities. Go visit.

Universal Cycling Links

♪♪♪ The List of Lists- another labor of love.

Chapter 13

Regional Resources

Beyond the hundreds of Internet cycling resources organized by topic, you'll find many more devoted to a specific region, whether a country, province, state, or city. These sites are often maintained by bicycle clubs in the area, though some serve as online tourist information centers. You can use these sites to plan a trip, contact cyclists in your area, or arrange to ride with new people while traveling. Some sites recommend places to stay, places to eat, and places to visit. Some offer local forecasts or summaries of seasonal climate; we've included a few comprehensive weather resources at the end of the chapter so you can plan ahead no matter where your bicycle takes you. Many general travel sites not listed in this chapter would also be excellent resources for cyclists planning a trip (try the InfoHub WWW Travel Guide at http://www.infohub.com or the Travel area on America Online).

We've listed only the addresses for these regional resources (and this list certainly isn't exhaustive!). Be sure to check Appendices B, C, and D for regional BBSs, newsgroups, and mailing lists. You can use a search engine (Chapter 12) to find Web sites for a specific location. You'll also find good regional ride information in the rec.bicycles.rides newsgroup, where you can also ask about specific tours and routes.

United States

Regional

Bike Northwest
http://www.accelerated.com/BikeNW/default.htm

Cycling the Pacific Northwest
http://hostel.com/~ebarnett/cyclepnw.html

Mid-Atlantic Cycling
gopher://gopher.voicenet.com/leisure/sports/cycling
http://www.voicenet.com/leisure/sports/cycling

Mountain Biking in the Western Rocky Mountains
http://www.microweb.com/rogm/single-tracks.html

National Park Service
http://www.nps.gov/nps/npsregion.html

New England Mountain Bike Association
http://www.ultranet.com/~kvk/nemba.html

New England Triathlon Page
http://www.cis.yale.edu/~jjankov/ne.html

North Atlantic Mountain Biking Race Calendar
http://www.toto.com:80/mpagano/pages/na/mtbneast.htm

Northwest Cycling Information Resource
http://www.eskimo.com/~cycling/echelon.html

Northwest Trilink
http://www.compumedia.com/~jewinter/welcome.html

Ride Midwest
http://team.teamnet.net/~ricko

Route 66
http://www.cs.kuleuven.ac.be/~swa/route66/main.html

Alaska

Bicycle Touring in Alaska
http://www.iceonline.com/home/roberb7/WWW/bcakfaq.html

Arizona

Dawn to Dust Mountain Bike Club
http://www.primenet.com/~tomheld/dd.htm

Mountain Biking
http://www.primenet.com/~bikeboy/az_mtb.html

California

Bike Racing in Northern California
http://www-graphics.stanford.edu/~cek/racing/racing.html

Cal Hiking and Outdoor Society (CHAOS)
http://www.emf.net/~chaos

Caltech Bicycle Club
http://www.cco.caltech.edu/~cycling/cycling.html

Grizzly Peak Cyclists (Berkeley)
http://www.vix.com/gpc

Lake Tahoe Mountain Biking
http://www.rahul.net:80/yaws/tahoe/mbike.html

Major Taylor Cycling Club (East Palo Alto)
http://catalog.com/bayside/mtcc/

Orange County MTB Page
http://metro.turnpike.net/rlawrenc/cycling.htm

Ranchos Cycling Club (San Diego)
http://coyote.csusm.edu/public/medeiros/cycle.html

Russian River
http://spiderweb.com/rrcocom/

Sacramento Wheelmen
http://www.xmission.com/~gastown/wheelmen/

San Diego Bicycling Page
http://www.qualcomm.com/users/srram/biking/sdbike.html

Santa Barbara Bicycle Coalition
http://www.rain.org/~gwissman/sbbc.html

Santa Rosa Cycling Club
http://grimmy.santarosa.edu:80/~bscherf/srcchomepage.html

Stanford Cycling Team
http://www-leland.stanford.edu/group/cycling

Tour d' Aliso Viejo (Orange County)
http://infopages.com/tour/

UCSD Cycling Team (San Diego)
http://llefkowitz.extern.ucsd.edu/ucsdbike.html

Velo Allegro Cycling Club (Long Beach)
http://www.earthlink.net/~mikeburk/velo.html

Yosemite National Park
http://www.compugraph.com/yosemite/index.html

Colorado

BCN Bicycle Center (Bolder)
http://bcn.boulder.co.us/transportation/bike.page.html

Colorado Mountain Bike Racing
http://www.tcinc.com/~mtbike/co_mtb.html

Crested Butte Online
http://www.cbinteractive.com/cbws/index.html
http://www.gunnison.com/cbutte/cbmtb.html

Durango Biking Trails
http://web.frontier.net/SCAN/ihbc/trails.html

Front Range Cycling
http://www.lance.colostate.edu/~jenine/bike/frbike.html

Rocky Mountain Cycling Club
http://www.hemi.com/~rmcc

District of Columbia

ChainLink (MTB)
http://apollo.gmu.edu/~chain/

Potomac Pedalers Touring Club
http://blueridge.infomkt.ibm.com/bikes/clubs/PPTC/PPTC.html

Washington D.C. and General Bicycling Information
http://www.access.digex.net/~buglady/bike_info.html

Whole Wheel Velo Club
http://www.dgsys.com/~rthonen/wwvc.html

Florida

Brevard County Cycling Center
http://www.digital.net/~charry/

MTB Florida
http://www.unf.edu/students/byoung/

Orlando Triathlon
http://www.magicnet.net/~csutton/tri.html

Tallahassee on 2Wheels
http://nsns.com:80/BigRing/2Wheels.html

Georgia

Atlanta Mountain Biking
http://www.mindspring.Com/~mike1/bike.html

Georgia Bicycle Federation
http://www.geopages.com/CapitolHill/1399

Southern Off-Road Bicycle Association
http://www.intergate.net/uhtml/sorba.html

Hawaii

Hawaii Bicycling League
http://www.pixi.com/~dsherman/HBL.html

Illinois

Joliet Bicycle Club
http://www.justnet.com/jbc

Indiana

Central Indiana Bicycle Association
http://a1.com/mstreet/ciba.html

Mountain Biking in Bloomington
http://ezinfo.ucs.indiana.edu/~adpeters/mtb/intro.html

Pedestrian/Bikeways Committee (Notre Dame/Saint Mary's College)
http://www.nd.edu/~ktrembat/www-bike/

Iowa

Iowa State University Mountain Bike Association
http://www.public.iastate.edu/~caweldon/isumba.html

Kansas

Biking Across Kansas
http://www.nets.com/bakintro.html

Kansas City Mountain Biking
http://www.primenet.com/~clemon

Kentucky

Louisville Wheelmen
http://www.merrickind.com/louwheel/

Louisiana

New Orleans Bicycle Club
http://www.gnofn.org/~nobc/

Maine

Acadia National Park by Bicycle
http://barharbor.com/anpbike.html

Sunday River Ski Resort
http://www.nxi.com/WWW/sunday_river/mountain.html

Maryland

Annapolis Bicycle Club
http://access5.digex.net:80/~mvore/abc.html

College Park Bicycle Club
http://www.glue.umd.edu/~naru/cpbc.html

Cycle Across Maryland
http://dcs.umd.edu/~clay/cam.html
410-653-2507 (BBS)

Massachusetts

Bicycle Coalition of Massachusetts (Mass Bike)
http://tdc-www.harvard.edu/bicycle/

Bicycle Information (MIT)
http://www.mit.edu:8001/people/baspitz/Bicycle/bicycle.html

Nashoba Valley Pedalers (Acton)
http://www.ultranet.com/~drjames/NVP.html

Northeast Bicycle Club (Bedford)
http://world.std.com/~nebikclb/index.html

Tufts Cycling Team
http://www.tufts.edu/~mabramso/bike.html

Westy's Cycling Page (Amherst)
http://eksl-www.cs.umass.edu/~westy/cycling.html

Michigan

Ann Arbor Velo Club
http://www.umich.edu/~ggood/aavc/

Minnesota

Dan's Cycling Page
http://att2.cs.mankato.msus.edu/~superdan/cycling.html

Flat City Cycling Club (Minneapolis/St. Paul)
ttp://www-mount.ee.umn.edu/FCCC/

Minnesota Mountain Biking Page
http://www.umn.edu/nlhome/m072/gjerd004/biking.html

Mississippi

Millsaps Bike Club
http://www.millsaps.edu/~kingst/bike.html

Missouri

Bike Columbia
http://www.sar.usf.edu/~hilderbr/trails/trails.html

Kansas City Mountain Biking
http://www.primenet.com/~clemon

Outdoor Activities in St. Louis
http://www.st-louis.mo.us/st-louis/outdoors.html

Montana

Cycling in the Rocky Mountains (Missoula)
http://ftp.cs.umt.edu/CS/FAC/wilde/Cycling/Cycling.html

Nebraska

Nebraska Recreation Trails
http://ngp.ngpc.state.ne.us/infoeduc/trails.html

New Hampshire

New Hampshire Mountain Biking Association
http://mmm.dartmouth.edu/pages/user/taa/bike.html

New Jersey

FreeWheelin
http://mv2.pupress.princeton.edu/
http://freewheelin.pupress.princeton.edu/

Jersey Shore Touring Society & Bicycle Club
http://www.att.com/JSTS/

New Jersey Mountain Biking
http://haven.ios.com/~karpk/bike/bike.shtml

NJ Online Biking
http://www.nj.com/bike/

Princeton Mountain Biking
http://www.princeton.edu/~jjroman/bike.html

New Mexico

Los Alamos
http://nis-www.lanl.gov/~pawel/bike.html

Project New Mexico
http://www.nmt.edu:80/~bridge/project_nm/project_nm.html

New York

Cycling on Long Island
http://www.webscope.com/li/cycling.html

EBikes (New York City)
gopher://gopher.panix.com/11/ebikes

New York Cycle Club
http://interport.net/~ckran/nycc.html

New York Cycling Home Page
http://www.cc.columbia.edu/~adr5/cycnyc1.html

Queens Mountain Biker
http://www.mtii.com:80/queens/chris.html

Rochester Bicycle Club
http://www.win.net/~rbcbbs
716-265-3357 (BBS)

Sleepy Hollow Bicycle Club (Westchester County)
http://www.shbc.org/shbc/home.html

Western New York Mountain Bicycling Association
http://128.205.166.43/public/wnymba/wnymba.html

North Carolina

North Carolina's Mountain Bike Page
http://www4.ncsu.edu/eos/users/c/ctgreen/www/Mountain.html

NC Fats Mountain Bike Club (Raleigh)
http://www4.ncsu.edu/unity/users/c/cadail/www/bike.html

Tarwheels Cycling Club (Durham)
http://www.cs.duke.edu/~carla/tarwheels.html

Ohio

Cycling in Columbus
http://www.aiinet.com/~kenh/cmh-cycle.html

Ohio University Mountain Bike Club
http://linus.cs.ohiou.edu/~mountain

Oklahoma

Sooner Pearl BMX Raceway
http://www.ionet.net/~bwgreen/sooner.shtml

Oregon

Bicycling in Eugene
http://www.efn.org/~sgazette/bicycles.html

Coghead Corner (Portland MTB)
http://www.teleport.com/~bazzle/coghead.shtml

Cycle Oregon Bicycle Tour
http://www.mmgco.com/pjp/cycleor.html

Southern Oregon Cycling Association
http://id.mind.net/~gumby/
503-734-2544 (BBS)

Team Oregon (Portland)
http://www.cse.ogi.edu/~walpole/team_oregon.html

Pennsylvania

CMU Explorers Mountain Bike Trailhead
http://cirque.edrc.cmu.edu:8008/mbike_front.html

Panther Cycling Team (Pittsburgh)
http://www.pitt.edu/~cycling/PCC/Home

Philadelphia Cycling
http://www.voicenet.com/philly/leisure/sports/cycling/

Pittsburgh Cycling Page
http://www.cs.cmu.edu/afs/cs.cmu.edu/user/jdg/www/bike/

University of Pennsylvania Cycling Club/Team
http://dolphin.upenn.edu:80/~pacebike

Tennessee

Appalachian Mountain Bike Club (Knoxville)
http://users.aol.com/ambc/ambchome.htm

Murfreesboro Bicycle Club
http://www.nashville.com/wws1154/mbc.html

Nashville Net Cycling
http://www.Nashville.Net/~cycling/

Texas

Bicycling in Houston
http://rampages.onramp.net/~pbeavers/bicycle.html

Dallas-Fort Worth Area Cycling
http://rampages.onramp.net/~tbarker/cycle.htm

Mountain Biking Austin
http://www.actlab.utexas.edu/~captain/mt.bike.html

North Texas Mountain Biking
http://www.unt.edu/~tjb0002/

San Antonio Wheelmen
http://www.cains.com/wheelmen/

Texas A&M Cycling Team
http://bush.cs.tamu.edu/~dbrenner/team_home.html

Utah

Outdoor Adventures—Bicycling
http://www.netpub.com/utah/utahadv/outdoor/uaoabicy.htm

Utah Mountain Biking
http://137.65.44.169:9000/

Vermont

Mountain Biking
http://together.net/~erik/vtmb/

Mountain Biking in Northern Vermont
http://salus.med.uvm.edu/mtb.html

Vermont Fat Tire Club
http://www.together.com/~erik/vftc/

Virginia

Eastern Virginia Mountain Biking
http://www.pinn.net/~wosborg/bike_hm.html

Mountain Biking Club of Virginia Tech
http://www.pinn.net/~vkrebs/cycling/cycling.html

Reston Web
http://townweb.com/herndon/sports/sports.html

Spinning Wheel
http://turnpike.net/metro/W/Winston/index.htm

Virginia Cycling Association
http://reality.sgi.com/employees/billh_hampton/vacycling/

Washington

Backcountry Bicycle Trails Club
http://www.compumedia.com/~agb/bbtc

B.I.K.E.S. Club—Snohomish County Bike Club
http://www.eskimo.com/~gorts/bikes.html

Cascade Bicycle Club (Seattle)
http://cascade.org/cbc.html

Metro Bicycling Information (King County)
http://transit.metrokc.gov/bike/bike.html

Mountain Biking in Port Townsend
http://www.olympus.net/personal/stevesch/mtn-bike.html

Pazzo Velo Team (Seattle)
http://www.kent.wednet.edu/ksd/it/brent/pazzo.html

Puget Sound Cycling Club
http://www.eskimo.com/~ambler/pscc.html

Team Washington
http://mindlink.net/luis_bernhardt/teamwa.html

University of Washington (Husky) Cycling Team
http://weber.u.washington.edu/~tongcoec

Wheelsport Cycling Team
http://www.wolfe.net/~cyclist/whlsport.html

WSDOT Bicycling
http://www.wsdot.wa.gov/ppsc/bike/

West Virginia

Bike West Virginia
http://www.cs.wvu.edu/usr07/parks/bike/biking_wv.html

Wisconsin

Bicycling Community Page (Madison/Dane County)
http://www.cs.wisc.edu/~condon/sd.html

Wyoming

Bike the Bighorns
http://wave.sheridan.wy.us/~btech/bikepage.html

Canada

Atlantic Canada Cycling Information
http://fox.nstn.ca/~cycling/AtlCanCycling.html

Bicycle Touring in British Columbia, Yukon, & Northwest Territories
http://www.iceonline.com/home/roberb7/WWW/bcakfaq.html

Canadian Cycling WWW
http://www.interlog.com/~bicycle/cycling.htm

The Cybernetic, Cycloidal, Cycling Source (Alberta)
http://www.cuug.ab.ca:8001/~gluzmana/

Edmonton Bicycle and Touring Club
gopher://freenet.edmonton.ab.ca/11/i/bicycle

Edmonton Bicycle Commuter Homepage
http://www.ualberta.ca/~vccheng/ebc.html

Mountain Biking in Quebec
http://www.infobahnos.com/~swsmith

New Brunswick
http://www.csi.nb.ca/tourism/page8.html

Newfoundland and Labrador
http://web.cs.mun.ca/~jamie/bnl/

One Less Car (Toronto)
http://olc.ismcan.com/
gopher olc.ismcan.com:70
416-480-0147 (BBS)

Ontario Coalition for Better Cycling
http://www.globalx.net/ocbc

Ontario MTB Pages
http://www.sunnybrook.utoronto.ca:8080/~jbishop/omtb.html

Ottawa Bicycle Club
http://www.sce.carleton.ca/rads/greg/obc/obc.html

Ottawa Cycling SIG (special interest groups)
http://www.ncf.carleton.ca/freeport/sigs/sports/cycling/menu
telnet 134.117.1.25

Prince Edward Island
http://www.gov.pe.ca/info/vg/out.html

Promo-Velo (Quebec)
http://www.uquebec.ca/Serveurs/RES/pv/pv.html [in French]

Quebec Biking Information
http://www.accent.net/jdoucet/index.html

Team Instrumar Cycling Home Page (St. John's, Newfoundland)
http://www.infonet.st-johns.nf.ca/providers/team-instrumar/

Vancouver Bicycle Club
http://www.iceonline.com/home/roberb7/WWW/vbc.html

Mexico

Xtreme- Ciclismo de Montaña
http://spin.com.mx/~aquirarte/mntbike.html [in Spanish]

Europe/Northern Asia

Europe
European Cyclists' Federation
http://www.oslonett.no/home/slf-bike/ecf.html

Europole
http://dafne.mines.u-nancy.fr/~europole/ [in French]
http://dafne.mines.u-nancy.fr/~europole~a.html [in German]
http://dafne.mines.u-nancy.fr/~europole/europole~e.html [in English]

Trento Bike Pages
http://www-math.science.unitn.it/Bike/

Austria

Austria
http://www.ifs.univie.ac.at/austria/ti.html [in German & English]

Wiener Mountainbike Seite
http://stud1.tuwien.ac.at/~e9125165/mtb/index.html [in German]

Denmark

Mountain Biking in Denmark
http://www.astro.ku.dk/~sune/dab/Mountainbike.html

Germany

Allgemeiner Deutscher Fahrrad Club
http://www.informatik.uni-trier.de/~bern/ADFC/ [in German]

German MTB Home Page
http://users.aol.com/gechoHH/ [in German]

Mountain Bike Guide
http://129.187.42.3/~betty/mtb/mtb.htm [in German]

Ireland

Irish Cycle Racing
http://iol.ie/~sshortal/index.html

Italy

Testata Giornalistica Sportiva
http://www.vol.it/raitgs/ [in Italian]

Touring Club Italiano
http://fs003mi.iol.it/tci.sdp/html/eindex.htm [in Italian]

The Netherlands

Bicycling Lane Along the Digital Highway (fietspad langs de disgitale snelweg)
http://www.dds.nl:80/~michiel/fiets/ [in Dutch]

Holland Tourist Information
http://www.nbt.nl/holland/bicycle/home.htm

Human Power Race Paris-Amsterdam (Web site at the Digital City of Amsterdam)
http://www.dds.nl/~paam

Rob's Mountainbike Page
http://www.xs4all.nl/~rcoende/index.html

WTOS - The Delft Student Cycling Club
http://dutcu15.tudelft.nl/~geert/wtoshome.htm

Norway

Jørn's Cycling Homepage
http://www.fysel.unit.no/dahls/cycling.html

Norwegian Cyclists' Association
http://www.oslonett.no/home/slf-bike/english.html

Portugal

Mountain Biking
http://www.coma.sbg.ac.at/~salchegg/MTBinP

Sweden

Blekholmstorget International Mountain Bikers
http://www.bahnhof.se/~ina/bleto/

Mike's Mountain Bike Pages (European MTB e-zine)
http://www.datastugan.se/mike/mtb/

Swedish Cycling Page
http://www.ludd.luth.se/~mange/

Ukraine

Kiev Local Bike Routes
http://www.lucky.net/~vt/private/biketours.shtml

United Kingdom

Bristol Cycling Campaign
http://zen.btc.uwe.ac.uk/~canute/bike.html

Central London CTC Rides
http://www.ma.ic.ac.uk/~apmath/clondonctc

University of Essex Mountain Bike Club
http://hcslx1.essex.ac.uk/~pdyson/Cycling/MBSX/

University of Southampton Bike User Network
http://www.soton.ac.uk/~ekg/bun.html

Pacific/Southeast Asia

Australia

Australian Capital Territory Government
http://actg.canberra.edu.au/actg/dus/csg/org9/org9.htm#bicycle

Cycling!
http://public-www.pi.se/~orbit/cycling.html

Phillip's Home Page
http://ilios.eng.monash.edu.au/~phillip/

Photo Album (Victoria, Melbourne)
http://werple.mira.net.au/~margaret/cycle.htm

Skyhigh (BMX in Western Australia)
http://www.iinet.net.au/~primus/

Tasmania
http://public-www.pi.se/~orbit/tas.html

Japan

Cycling Around Aizu-Wakamatsu
http://castor.u-aizu.ac.jp/Circles/Bicycle/bicycle-circle.html

New Zealand

Mountain Biking
http://hmu1.cs.auckland.ac.nz:80/5708389D/Cmtbnz

Mountain Bike Web
http://www.wcc.govt.nz/extern/kennett/homepage.htm

Web Travel Review
http://www-swiss.ai.mit.edu/philg/new-zealand/

Vietnam

Cycle Vietnam
http://192.253.114.31/Misc/Vietnam/Cycle_Vietnam_-_Cover_Page.html

Africa

South Africa

South African Cycling
http://www.aztec.co.za/users/dcowie

Weather Resources

Integrated Earth Information Server
http://atm.geo.nsf.gov/ieis/weather.html
gopher atm.geo.nsf.gov

University of Illinois Weather Machine
gopher://wx.atmos.uiuc.edu:70/1/

WeatherNet
http://cirrus.sprl.umich.edu/wxnet/

Chapter 14

Rules of the Road

Cycling in cyberspace is not as dull or one-sided as you might imagine. You're not just typing away on your computer. You're interacting with other people through computers. In fact, because sending messages electronically is so fast, it is more like conversation than correspondence. Sometimes this is hard to remember, though. The imagery described in this chapter may be useful to keep in mind whenever you sign on.

Meeting Other Cyclists

Before you venture onto the information superhighway, picture yourself on a paved road or bike path. Consider how you want other drivers and path users to treat you: with courtesy and respect. You should be ready to do the same for fellow travelers in cyberspace. Remember, you're sharing the road with millions of other people who can and will see how you behave online.

If you're joining a discussion group (a live chat session, a mailing list, or a newsgroup), keep the mental image of talking to other people face-to-face in, say, a bike shop. You wouldn't interrupt without listening to the conversation first and taking note of the different participants. You wouldn't ask a question that someone else had just asked. You wouldn't listen to useful advice from the mechanic and walk away without thanking him or her. You wouldn't laugh at a new rider. You wouldn't scorn the stories of an experienced veteran. You wouldn't use abusive language in front of a child.

Remember too that wherever you go online, the Internet and other networks are international. Cultures, perspectives, and languages are different. Even English is different. Be sensitive to all these factors and more when greeting your fellow global cyclists online. How well would you do asking about a derailleur adjustment in Mandarin?

Online Body Language

Conversing online is made a little easier by the use of emoticons and other keyboard shortcuts. You can show some body language online by inserting one of these symbols occasionally:

: -) (smile)	; -) (wink)	: -D (laugh)
: - ((frown)	: -o (surprise)	: -/ (skeptical)

You'll also see lots of typed art in signature files, such as the cyclist cruising across the top of the pages throughout this book. Online mountain bikers and triathletes have pushed the Courier font to its creative limits.

Other shortcuts are used to make invisible and unformatable communication a little easier to follow. Some folks use <g> as shorthand for grin. You'll see _urgency_ or *emphasis* placed with some sort of mark on either side of the stressed word. All capital letters are reserved for SHOUTING and are considered rude otherwise (except when used by disabled individuals whose computer setup requires all caps). You can cut down on the amount of typing and verbiage with several acronyms:

BTW (by the way)   IMHO (in my humble opinion)

FYI (for your information)   YMMV (your mileage may vary)

TIA (thanks in advance)   TIC (tongue in cheek)

FS (for sale)   WTB (wanted to buy)

ROTFL (rolling on the floor laughing)

TIOOYK (There Is Only One You Know—refers to the Tour de France)

You'll quickly realize why some sort of typed body language is so critical. You may have heard about "flaming" or "flame wars"—angry, online accusations and arguments. Flames hurt everyone. One hasty, thoughtless comment by a participant can ruin his or her online reputation. Nonparticipants (in the flames) find their group cluttered with people shouting at each other, and they usually don't like the waste of time and space. They may at times feel like an embarrassed house guest caught between dueling spouses.

If you decide to respond to a comment or piece of advice offered online, use utmost diplomacy and consider what the words on the screen—not all the untyped words in your head—actually say. You may want to add a "no flame intended" note to diffuse any angry reactions to your opposing point of view (this is assuming you do not intend to flame someone). Put yourself back in that imaginary bike shop: you'd be pretty careful how you made your suggestion to the former Hell's Angel who gave some incorrect instructions for truing a wheel. Sarcasm is even harder to detect on an expressionless computer screen than it is on a straight-faced cynic. Finally, remember that some people just like to argue, not necessarily in a mean-spirited fashion.

Joining the Conversation

Long discussions (also known as "threads"), whether or not they involve flames, usually involve quoting from previous messages to keep everything in context. Some people use colons at the start of each line of quoted material, while others merely indent the reprinted text. Most of the time you'll see a series of > symbols, with an additional > for each layer of quotes (many newsgroup readers insert these symbols automatically). For example:

```
>>>How else can I reduce my total body/bike weight?
>>... or an appendectomy would eliminate the
>>weight from one unnecessary body part.
>Unless the surgeon left a pair of forceps behind. ;-)
In which case you could afford a Lotus from
the proceeds of the lawsuit...
```

Yes, it can get involved, and you never know where a thread is headed. In this example, the bottom line (no > in front) is by the author of the current message, who is in turn quoting material from three previous messages. Normally the authors of the prior messages would also be named (including their e-mail addresses). If you spend more time on the bike than at the computer, you won't need to worry about these neverending threads. Among many circular discussions, the Campagnolo versus Shimano debate will never die.

Returning to the analogy of a local bike shop, if you visited frequently, you would get to know the regulars. You'd form opinions of them in your own mind and listen more closely to some people than to others. Would you take advice—especially if it sounded a bit sensational—from a stranger who had just walked in? You'd probably at least discuss it with the regulars whom you trusted. Do the same online. Just because it's on the computer doesn't mean it's true. (Be especially wary of anyone complaining about a specific bike shop or person—you'll never know all the details.) See what other people have to say and feel free to share your own experience with a particular component or trail if it is relevant to the discussion.

I have found an interesting mix of fact and fiction on the Internet that arises from the peculiarities of human nature. I learned early that many people speak authoritatively about things they profess to understand although they don't. Still, it amazes me how much hearsay and unfounded information is presented on the Net. The same was true before the Internet, when the flow of myth and lore came from magazine articles and bicycle shops. Bicycle wheels were a favorite topic, so much so, that I wrote "the Bicycle Wheel" to stem that tide.

The Internet, like television, has tremendous potential for information, but it requires a discriminating viewer to select useful information. It requires an ability to detect who is presenting accurate information and who is posturing with myth and lore clothed in jargon.

Jobst Brandt, jbrandt@hpl.hp.com

Speaking Up

Suppose you want to start a conversation or ask a question. First, you need to be sure you're talking to the right group. Some newsgroup readers allow you to "cross-post" messages, which means that your note is sent to several newsgroups at once. In fact, you can tell the whole world just about anything, but you won't make any friends that way. Target your posts to the right group. You'll know which group is right after you follow the conversation for a few days or a week.

Online, your subject line is the ice breaker. You want to keep it short and focused but not to the point of ambiguity. For example, `SunTour BB` could be a question, an opinion, or an announcement about this component. If you're asking a question, include a question mark at the end to show inflection. For example, `SunTour BB Repair Needed ?` will attract the attention of people who know how to fix a bottom bracket; otherwise, anyone who owns a SunTour bottom bracket may read the note thinking there has been a recall or other warning (of course, messages about recalls should say so in the subject line).

In addition, be as specific as necessary. Sending the message entitled only `Riding Partner Needed` might be appropriate in a local group, such as in Philadelphia or San Francisco, but not in the internationally read groups. You'll realize the importance of carefully worded subject lines after you wade through several that *sounded* interesting and bypass even more that are too vague to catch your attention. If you've got a lot to say, include a polite `(long)` or `(long post)` in your subject line.

What's too long? You're life history of cycling probably falls into that category. But so do many rambling responses. In a conversation with a crowd of people (back to the bike shop again), you wouldn't speak in paragraphs.

The cycling community on the Usenet is pretty amazing. There is really no need to go anywhere other than Usenet for information on bicycle maintenance, race reports, and rides. The real limitation of Usenet is that past discussions do not get archived. Each newsgroup has at least one helmet war per year; rec.bicycles.racing has a professional drug use discussion over and over again. These repetitive threads lower the signal-to-noise ratio, which makes life more difficult for everyone. New users should watch and read for several weeks before posting a message. Never enter a flame war without an asbestos suit, and be prepared to back up anything you say with direct evidence. You will almost certainly get more out of Usenet than you put in (unless your name is Roger Thomas).

Dave Blake, dblake@bme.jhu.edu

You'd respond in a sentence or two or summarize your opinion briefly and to the point. If you wanted to talk to one or two people at length about a particular topic or share your personal experience, you'd do that separately from the main group. Online, you would do this via direct e-mail correspondence instead of in the newsgroup or on the mailing list. Remember, some people may still be paying by the word to read what you have to say.

What if no one responds to your message? If you made a comment, people may have read it and nodded to themselves without doing anything else. If you asked a question, it may have been too vague or broad, such as `how do I get a wheel back in true?` A potential reader would be wondering what kind of wheel (road, off-road, aero, or other specialty wheel), how bad the problem is, whether you had an accident or the problem arose gradually, and so on. On the other hand, you may have a question that is so individualized that no one reading your message has sufficient expertise to respond.

If you ask a common question, you may be told to read the group's FAQ (remember, this is the frequently asked questions file, which answers many common queries raised in the newsgroup); of course, you should do this first anyway. You may be directed to a particular Web site for more information. If you specifically ask where on the Internet to go for specific help, you'll probably get a few suggestions, either posted in the group or sent to you privately via e-mail. You'll almost certainly get an opinion if you ask about a specific component, a complete bike, or a particular ride.

Of course, no one is obligated to respond at all. Like you, other cybercyclists have jobs or course work and families and friends to tend to (not to mention their bikes). You'll find, though, that the online cycling community is very dynamic and supportive. Just remember to mind your manners and send thank-you notes.

Based on personal experience, I would recommend that people be careful of the information that is available on the Net. There are rumors, mistruths, jokes, leg-pullings, and all other kinds of stuff that the inexperienced cyclist/ netter could take the wrong way. Once you've been online for a while, you learn to weed out the people whose advice you take with a grain of salt from those who give accurate information. It's amazing the number of "answers," true and otherwise, you can get to a single question. Avoid answers that start out with "I know a guy who..." or "I heard...." Of course, this is no different from the real world except that most people place more credibility in something they see in print....

Pete Ruckelshaus, mudboy@astro.ocis.temple.edu

Even The Information Superhighway Has Potholes...

Sometimes you may have difficulty reaching a particular destination on the Internet. Error messages and slow connections may become more frequent as more and more people come online. However, we can suggest a few tips to try before you become too frustrated:

- If you can't reach a resource, don't give up. Try again later or another day. The computer at that site may be having temporary problems or be disconnected from the Internet for preventive maintenance. Popular sites may be sluggish because so many people are using them.

- If a site has moved, the owners will usually leave the URL and a link (pointer) to the new address. If not, consult Chapter 12 to learn how to find the new URL.

- You may get a message that the URL entered does not exist. Check to see that you have typed in the URL exactly as written, including all capital letters and punctuation. If possible, try to access the site with Netscape, the most widely used browser (it's able to read just about every Web page, which isn't true for other browsers), or a text browser, such as Lynx.

- If you have trouble connecting to the full address, try using only the first portion. For example, if the address

  http://galaxy.einet.net/galaxy/Leisure-and-Recreation/Sports/Biking.html

  gives you trouble, just use

  http://galaxy.einet.net/galaxy/

  and then work your way through the appropriate directories (the words between the slashes should give you clues if not the actual names) to get to the Biking section of Galaxy.

- If absolutely nothing is happening, wait at least five minutes before you cancel the connection. Making Internet connections around the world can take a long time, especially during prime hours (roughly 7 A.M. to 7 P.M. Eastern time in the United States). In the evening, heavy consumer use and scheduled conferences jam many commercial services. Again, popular sites may have the maximum number of users signed on.

- Online resources are constantly evolving—always "under construction." If a particular site disappoints you, check again later and you may find a wealth of information and support.

- Finally, remember that you can be held legally accountable for what you post online. Although the Internet is international, and the laws governing it are still being shaped, use common sense and courtesy in cyberspace. Be careful about copyright infringement (request permission to post anything written or created by someone else) and libel (a false statement about someone that causes injury to his or her reputation).

Common Abbreviations

In this book, we've tried to use only the most ubiquitous abbreviations that you'll find online. These are summarized below with very basic explanations. If you really want to learn the alphabet soup of Net-speak, we would once again recommend that you spend some time browsing (offline, in your library or bookstore) through Internet reference books until you find a volume that matches your level of expertise and interest.

BBS = Bulletin Board System (a computer you can access with a modem)

FAQ = Frequently Asked Questions (a single document answering many common questions related to a central topic)

FTP = File Transfer Protocol (protocol—or rules—used for transferring files from computer to computer)

HTML = HyperText Mark-up Language (programming language used to construct Web pages—often pronounced HoT MetaL)

HTTP = HyperText Transport Protocol (protocol for Web surfing)

IRC = Internet Relay Chat (real-time, live conversations held at a virtual central site among people around the world)

QWK = software used to download and read mail/messages from BBSs (will save you time online and often money)

URL = Universal Resource Locator (Internet address)

WWW = World Wide Web (multimedia portion of Internet, browsed through hypertext links)

Organizations Online

Many bicycle organizations and clubs now use online resources to help carry out their mission. Several of the groups listed below have been discussed in appropriate chapters. More organizations have come online since this book was written, so be sure to use Lycos or WebCrawler to check for a particular group not listed here or reviewed earlier. Regional groups, such as state bicycle federations in the United States, may have URLs listed in Chapter 13 or mailing lists at VeloNet (see Appendix D for list).

Adventure Cycling Association
ACABike@AOL.com
http://web2.starwave.com/outside/online/organization/adv/main.html

Bicycle Federation of America
BikeFed@aol.com

Bicycle Federation of Australia
bicycle@ozemail.com
http://www.ozemail.com.au/~bicycle/

European Cyclists' Federation
arild@oslonett.no
http://www.oslonett.no/home/slf-bike/ecf.html

International Christian Cycling Club
mle7@aol.com

International Federation of Cycle Messengers and Companies
http://ourworld.compuserve.com/homepages/IFCMC/

International Human Powered Vehicle Association
MARTID@aol.com
http://ihpva.org/

International Mountain Bicycling Association
IMBA@aol.com
http://www.outdoorlink.com/IMBA

League of American Bicyclists
dwtlaw@aol.com
http://www.clark.net/pub/league/homepage.htm

National Off-Road Bicycling Association
http://www.adventuresport.com/asap/norba/norba.html

Professional Bicycle League
http://www.drop-in.com/pbl

United States Cycling Federation
USCFMember@aol.com

Bulletin Board Systems

You can use almost any local BBS to access the BikeNet echo (discussion group) available through FidoNet and/or the Usenet newsgroups listed in Appendix C. If none of your local BBSs carry any cycling message areas (and a polite request to the sysop to add the BikeNet echo comes up empty), you can try one of the BBSs listed below to access bicycle-related discussions, software, graphics, and classified ads. This list is clearly not exhaustive, but you'll find friendly cyclists at these sites who may be able to point you to a bicycle-oriented BBS closer to home. For help signing on and using a BBS, refer back to Chapter 1.

Bicycle Bulletin Board
619-720-1830 [Carlsbad, CA]

BikeWeb
508-792-2881 [Worcester, MA]

CyberCircle
210-661-5417 [San Antonio, TX]

CycleNet
617-224-9808 [Wakefield, MA]

One Less Car
416-480-0147 [Toronto, ON]

Rochester Bicycling Club
716-265-3357 [Rochester, NY]

Southern Oregon Cycling Association
503-734-2544 [Ashland, OR]

Tour de France
416-690-8121 [Scarborough, ON]

Tranquility Base
210-699-1710 [San Antonio, TX]

Turning Point
512-703-4400 [Austin, TX]

Wheel Werks
619-729-2884 [Carlsbad, CA]

Appendix C

Usenet Newsgroups

Usenet newsgroups are one of the most important online resources for cyclists. The international newsgroups bring together a wealth of advice, experience, news, and opinions. Local groups offer the added benefit of announcing rides, posting classified ads, and arranging cycling events (only a very few of those available are listed here). Since this book was written, a rec.bicycles.BMX newsgroup may have been launched; proposed groups for downhill and observed trials are less likely to come online. Be sure to read the rec.bicycles FAQ (see Chapter 4) for the latest Usenet newsgroup details.

Newsgroup	Focus
alt.mountain-bike	General discussions of mountain biking
aus.bicycles	Cycling in Australia
ba.bicycle	Cycling in the San Francisco Bay Area
bc.cycling	Cycling in British Columbia and Canada
bit.listserv.sportpsy	Discussion of sports psychology
dc.biking	Cycling in the Washington, DC, area
de.rec.fahrrad	General discussions of biking in Germany
fj.rec.bicycles	General discussions of biking in Asia
misc.fitness	Discussions of fitness and sports nutrition
phl.bicycles	Cycling in the Philadelphia area
rec.bicycles.marketplace	Buying, selling, and reviewing components
rec.bicycles.misc	Riding techniques, nutrition, injuries, etc.
rec.bicycles.offroad	Discussions of off-road riding, trail issues, etc.
rec.bicycles.racing	Bicycle racing results, schedules, rules, and tips
rec.bicycles.rides	Touring, organized rides, riding partners, etc.
rec.bicycles.soc	Commuting, advocacy, road hazards, etc.
rec.bicycles.tech	Design, construction, upgrades, repair, etc.
rec.sport.triathlon	Sport of triathlon (many cycling-related posts)
rec.sport.unicycling	Buying, riding, and enjoying unicycles
sci.med.nutrition	Scientific and clinical discussions of nutrition
uk.rec.cycling	Cycling in the United Kingdom
umich.biking	Cycling at the University of Michigan

Mailing Lists

Below you will find the name, subscription address (also used for routine tasks, such as unsubscribing or getting help), and discussion address (used for messages you want the entire group to read) for many cycling mailing lists. Refer back to Chapter 3 for general information on interacting with a mailing list. Lists that use Listproc or Listserv (instead of Majordomo) software have a slightly different subscription command: you include your full name at the end after subscribe and the list name. New lists are always being started, so you might want to check for other Internet mailing lists on Westy's Cycling Page (aka David Westbrook) at http://eksl-www.cs.umass.edu/~westy/cycling/cycling-on-internet.html and at several of the sites described in Chapter 12. The most important list, especially if you can't read Usenet newsgroups, is Bicycle (Chapter 4).

Mailing Lists Throughout the Internet

atb (mountain biking)
atb@cyc.net [subscribe atb *your name*]
extreme_atb@cycnet.com

bicycle (general discussion)
listproc@list.cren.net [subscribe bicycle *your name*]
bicycle@list.cren.net

bike (Cascade Bicycle Club)
majordomo@cortland.com [subscribe bike]
bike@cortland.com

bike (Philadelphia/Delaware Valley)
bike-request@bcdv.drexel.edu [subscribe bike *your name*]
bike@bcdv.drexel.edu

bike midwest
majordomo@fuji.physics.indiana.edu [subscribe bike midwest]
bikemidwest@fuji.physics.indiana.edu

bikevt (Vermont)
listserv@moose.uvm.edu [subscribe bikevt *your name*]
bikevt@moose.uvm.edu

citybikes (San Francisco area rides)
citybikes-request@eff.org [subscribe citybikes *your name*]
citybikes@eff.org

dcbike (Washington, DC/mid-Atlantic)

wsilverman@igc.apc.org [subscribe dcbike *your name*]
dcbike@igc.apc.org

ebikes (New York City)

ebikes-request@mailhost.panix.com [subscribe ebikes *your name*]
ebikes@panix.com

helmets (Bicycle Helmet Safety Institute)

helmets@bhsi.org [subscribe helmets *your name*]
helmets@bhsi.org

hpv (includes discussion of recumbents)

majordomo@ihpva.org
hpv@ihpva.org

massbike

massbike-request@cfa165.harvard.edu [subscribe massbike *your name*]
massbike@cfa165.harvard.edu

mtb

mystery-request@lunch.asd.sgi.com [subscribe mtb *your name*]
mtb@lunch.asd.sgi.com

mtn-bike (San Francisco Bay area)

mtn-bike-request@warp9.ebay.sun.com [subscribe mtn-bike *your name*]
mtn-bike@warp9.ebay.sun.com

sfbike (San Francisco)

davesnyder@igc.apc.org [subscribe sfbike *your name*]
sfbike@igc.apc.org

tandem

listserv@hobbes.ucsd.edu [subscribe tandem *your name*]
tandem@hobbes.ucsd.edu

tri-drs (Dead Runner Society triathletes)

listserv@listserv.dartmouth.edu
tri-drs@listserv.dartmouth.edu

unicycling

majordomo@winternet.com [subscribe unicycling]
unicycling@winternet.com

womens-cycling

listserv@netcom.com [subscribe womens-cycling *your name*]
womens-cycling@netcom.com

Mailing Lists on VeloNet *(majordomo@cycling.org)*

Be sure to check with VeloNet to get the latest list of mailing lists by visiting the Web page (http://cycling.org/mailing.lists/) or by sending an e-mail message to majordomo@cycling.org with `Lists` in the message body.

abc –Atlanta Bicycle Campaign, Atlanta, GA
actc – Almaden Cycle Touring Club, San Jose, CA
ambc – Appalachian Mountain Bike Club, Knoxville, TN
announce-de – Announcements in Delaware
av – Alto Velo Bicycle Racing Club, Palo Alto, CA
av-novice – Alto Velo Bicycle Racing Club/Novice, Palo Alto, CA

ba-announce – San Francisco Bay area alerts and announcements, CA
bbtc – Backcountry Bicycle Trails Club, WA
bcp – Bicycle Club of Philadelphia, Philadelphia, PA
bikecurrent – Discussions regarding bicycle electronics
bikeham – Cycling and amateur radio operation
bikemedic – Cycling and emergency medical services
bikepeople – General/international list for bicycle advocacy
bike-ms – Bicycling Mississippi, MS
bike-station – Bike commuter centers at transit stations
bmx – BMX race information, news, and discussion
bta-wa – Bicycle Transportation Alliance, Western Australia
btc-eastbay – Bicycle Trails Council of the East Bay, SF Bay Area, CA
btcm – Bicycle Trails Council of Marin, SF Bay Area, CA
bucc – British Universities Cycling Clubs, UK
burps – Bikers Under Rotary Pedaling Stress, UK

caboforum – California Association of Bicycling Organizations
caltrain-bikes – Bicycles on Caltrain, CA
cbc – California Bicycle Coalition, CA
cbsn-announce – California Bicycle Safety Network
ccmtb – Chester County mountain biking, PA
chinook – Chinook Cycling Club, WA
claire – Campaign for Clean Air and Exercise
coaching – Coaching discussions for racers
commute-logistics – Discussions regarding bicycle commuting logistics
crw – Charles River Wheelmen, Boston, MA
cucc – Cambridge University Cycling Club, UK

dbc – Davis Bike Club, Davis, CA
dc-tandems – Tandem enthusiasts in the Washington, DC, area

enduro-ba – Endurance riding/racing in the SF Bay area, CA
eurobike – General list for cyclists in Europe

facilities-n-planning – Transportation infrastructure affecting cycling
flcc – Finger Lakes Cycling Club, Ithaca, NY

gbc – Georgia Bicycle Federation, GA
gcc – Garden City Cyclists, Santa Clara, CA
gcc-fla – Gainsville Cycling Club, FL
ggtc – Golden Gate Triathlon Club, San Francisco, CA
go-events-uk – Great Outdoor Events, London, UK

hcmb – HardCore Canadian Mountain Bikers, Alberta, Canada
hellyer – Hellyer Park Velodrome events, San Jose, CA
helmet-standards – American Society for Testing Materials, USA

iccc – International Christian Cycling Club
icebike – General discussions about winter cycling
ifcmc – International Federation of Cycle Messengers and Companies

kycyclist – Louisville Wheelmen, KY

la-bac-news – Los Angeles Citizens Bicycle Advisory Committee, CA
la-sbbike – Los Angeles South Bay Bicycle Advocates, CA
lehigh – Lehigh Valley Road & Trail Cycling Club, PA
lgbrc – Los Gatos Bicycle Racing Club, CA
listowners – Forum for Majordomo list managers on cycling.org
lscc – Loughborough Students Cycling Club, UK

major-taylor – Major Taylor Cycling Club, East Palo Alto, CA
marketplace – Discussions regarding buying a bicycle or components
massbike – Bicycle Coalition of Massachusetts, MA
massbike-announce – Bicycle Coalition of Massachusetts announcements
masters – Discussions about masters racing (USCF & NORBA)
mbc – Milpitas Bicycle Club, CA
mcf – Minnesota Cycling Federation, MN
messengers – Bicycle messengers and couriers
michbike – League of Michigan Bicyclists, MI
midpen-patrol – MROSD Volunteer Trail Patrol, CA
more – Mid–Atlantic Off Road Enthusiasts, Washington, DC
mornride – The Morning Ride, Palo Alto, CA
mtb – General discussions about mountain biking
mtb-canada – Mountain biking in Canada
mtb-co – Mountain biking in Colorado, USA
mtb-new-england – Mountain biking in New England, USA
mtb-trials – Discussion of mountain bike trials riding
murt – Manchester University Racing Team, UK
mva – Marymoor Velodrome Association, WA

ncca-info – National Collegiate Cycling Association, USA
     accc-info – Atlantic Collegiate Cycling Conference
     ecc-info – Eastern
     mwccc-info – Midwest
     ncccc-info – North-Central
     nwccc-info – Northwest
     rmccc-info – Rocky Mountain
     scccc-info – South-Central
     seccc-info – Southeast
     swccc-info – Southwest
     wccc-info – Western
ncca-talk – Discussion list for NCCA, USA
ncnca – Northern Caliornia Nevada Cycling Association, NV/CA
ncnca-results – Race results for NCNCA
ncvc – National Capital Velo Club, Washington, DC
nesca – New England Cycling Support Association, USA
notable – NOrth Texas Alliance of Bicycle LEaders, TX
nsc – North Shore Cyclists, MA
nybc – New York Bicycling Coalition, NY

obc – Ottawa Bicycle Club, Ottawa, Ontario, Canada
occ – Onondaga Cycling Club, Syracuse, NY
ocsj – Outdoor Club of South Jersey, NJ
ohiobike – Forum for all cyclists in the state of Ohio
oucc – Oxford University Cycling Club, UK

pace – PENN Association of Cycling Enthusiasts, PA
patrol – General mountain bike patrol discussion group
pbc – Pennsylvania Bicycle Club, PA
pro-news – Professional cycling news
psycho – Psycho Psyclists, AZ

qcw – Quaker City Wheelmen, Philadelphia, PA

race-results – International, Cat A & US Pro race results
racing-us-nw – Racing in the Pacific Northwest, USA
randon – Randoneering (touring and noncompetitive ultradistance riding)
rbc – Rochester Bicycling Club, NY
road-canada – Road cycling in Canada
romp – Responsible Organized Mountain Pedalers, SF Bay Area, CA

saba – Sacramento Area Bicycle Advocates, CA
sacramento-wheelmen – Sacramento Wheelmen, CA
safety-n-education – Discussion of bike safety, education, and related issues
santa-cruz-bikes – Santa Cruz County Region, CA

sbw – South Broward Wheelers, FL
sccc – Sunnyvale/Cupertino Cycling Club, Sunnyvale/Cupertino, CA
scu – Suburban Cyclist Unlimited, PA
scw –South Chicago Wheelmen, Crete, IL
sdcbc – San Diego County Bicycle Coalition, CA
sdva – San Diego Velodrome Association, CA
sfbike – San Francisco Bicycle Coalition, CA
sf-critical-mass – Critical Mass rides and issues in San Francisco, CA
shucc – Sheffield Hallam University Cycling Club, Sheffield, UK
sjbc – San Jose Bicycle Club, San Jose, CA
sjbc-chat – San Jose Bicycle Club (chat list), San Jose, CA
skyline – Skyline Bicycle Club, Sunnyvale, CA
sportable – Sportable Racing Team, Ottawa, Canada
stbc – Southern Tier Bicycle Club, NY

tbc – Texas Bicycle Coalition, TX
team-internet – Discussion list for Team Internet
teamo – Discussion list for Team Oregon, OR
touring – General discussion of all aspects of bicycle touring
trifed-smw – Triathlon Federation, South Midwest, USA

ubcycling – University at Buffalo Cycling Club, NY
ultra – Discussions regarding ultramarathon cycling events
upenn – University of Pennsylvania Cycling Team, PA
urbancyclist-uk – Cycling in the cities of the United Kingdom
usaba – U.S. Association for Blind Athletes (Tandem Cycling Team), USA
uscf-district20 – USCF District 20 Association, MD-DE-DC-NoVA
uscf-district42 – USCF District 42 Association, VA
uscf-officials – US road and track bicycle race officiating
uscf-rap – Discussions regarding USCF, NORBA and US Pro racing
uscf-results – Race results for USCF events
uwacc – University of Western Australia Cycling Club

vbf – Virginia Bicycling Federation, VA
velodromes-us – Operators and promoters of velodromes in the US
velont-admin – Discussions regarding the operation of VeloNet

webmasters – Discussions among webmasters of cycling-related Web sites
wheelsport – Wheelsport Cycling Team, Kent, WA
whirl – Washington's Happily Independent Recumbent Lovers, DC
wild-sa – Women In Love with Dirt Cycling, South Africa
wnymba – Western New York Mountain Bicycling Association, NY
ww – Western Wheelers Bicycle Club, Palo Alto, CA
ww-chat – Western Wheelers Bicycle Club (chat list), Palo Alto, CA

Companies Online

You won't be surprised to learn that hundreds of companies involved in some aspect of cycling have established their presence online, either with an e-mail address through which you can contact customer service or a Web site where you can see new products, leave comments and questions, read reviews, and place orders. Because the Internet is constantly changing, even this list is not exhaustive, and many companies not listed here are available through AOL message centers. If you're looking for a particular company, try searching for it with Lycos, WebCrawler, or Yahoo (Chapter 12). Several of the commercial sites listed in Chapter 4, such as Cyber Cyclery, VeloLinQ, and Cycle Expo, also maintain long lists of industry contact information. Be sure to check Pete Ruckelshaus' BikIndex (Chapter 12) and Bike'alog (Chapter 8), too. In this appendix, companies that could fall under different categories are only listed once, so be sure to look through all the lists for your favorite product.

You may want to stop by CycleLink, the Bicycle Industry Organization (BIO) Web site (http://www.cyclelink.com/cycle). Here you'll find several companies (such as Pearl Izumi, QT, Inc., Softride, Thule), information about BIO's goals and Board of Directors, the current edition of BIOGraph (the industry newsletter), and several useful links. Separately, CycleNet offers a mailing list for people working in the bicycle industry (e-mail your request to join the discussion to administrator@cycnet.com).

Finally, be sure to be on the lookout for Dave Blake's R.B.T. Failures Compilation, a list of bicycles and components that have failed under normal or stressful use (user explains circumstances, including body weight, miles ridden, type of riding, etc.). You'll find this useful service in the rec.bicycles.tech newsgroup.

Bicycle Manufacturers/Frame Builders

Aegis
http://www.alpenglow.com/~cj/raceweb/aegis/AEGIS.html

Aerobike (recumbent)
http://www.strath.ac.uk/~cjbs23/aerobikes.html
100412.363@compuserve.com

Ancillotti Cycles
http://www.adventuresports.com/asap/shops/anciloti.htm

AMP Research
http://www.amp-research.com/
feike@amp-research.com

Arctos Machine (frame building)
lapdog@crl.com

Arrow Bicycles
http://www.accelerated.com:80/arrowracing/

Arvon Cycles
http://www.afternet.com/~arvon
arvon@afternet.com

Barracuda
dpon100@aol.com

Batavus Bicycles (in Dutch)
http://www.batavus.com/index.htm

BikeE
evol268707@aol.com

BMC Racing
http://www.bmc-racing.com/mtb
info@bmc-racing.com

Bontrager
bci@cruzio.com

Boulder Bicycles
http://cyclery.com/boulder_bikes

Brew Racing Frames
http:///cyclery.com/brew/index.html
Brew1dude@aol.com

Brompton (folding)
http://www.infoservice.com/brompton

Cambie Cycles (recumbent)
http://www2.portal.ca/~r-bent.htm
r-bent@portal.ca

Cannondale
http://www.cannondale.com/
CanDaleTch@aol.com
CanDaleCS@aol.com

Carbonframes
http://www.wsmith.com/veloling/carbfram/
maincarb.html
carbonbike@aol.com

CODA
CodaTS@aol.com
Coda96@aol.com

Conejo
http://cyclery.com/conejo

Easton (aluminum tubing)
kgladden@aol.com

Easy Racers, Inc. (recumbent)
http://www.armory.com/~zap/adverts/easy.html
tooeasy1@aol.com

Ellsworth Handcrafted Bicycles
http://cyclery.com/ellsworth/index.html
AnEllswrth@aol.com

Fat City Cycles
http://www.cyclelink.com/fatcity

Fisher Bicycle
http://www.fisherbikes.com

FutureCycles
http://www.demon.co.uk/history/cycles/
futurecycles.html

GT
http://www.gtbicycles.com/

Hujsak Custom Bicycles
http://www.internetnow.com/hujsak/index.html

Ibis
http://www.crl.com/~scot/
chuckibis@aol.com

Just Two Bikes (recumbent)
http://www.olympus.net/olympia/biz/jtb/jtb.html
muellner@halcyon.com
74771.2737@compuserve.com

KHS
http://cyclery.com/KHS/index.html
KHS@bikealog.com

Kona
jb595@aol.com

Marin Mountain Bikes
http://www.marinbikes.com/

McMahon Racing Cycles (MRC)
http://cyclery.com/MRC/index.html

Michals Design & Innovation
http://www.fractalboy.com/micals/
johnnyb1@ix.netcom.com

Moto-BMX
http://www.shadow.net/~victord/bmx.htm
VictorD@Shadow.net

Nexus Bicycle Company (folding)
http://world.std.com/~nexibike

Quintana Roo
http://www.webcom.com/~rooworld
QRman@cts.com

Raleigh USA (and Nishiki)
Raleighbik@aol.com

Recreation Industries (SeaCycle)
http://www.islandnet.com/~seacycle/
seacycle.html
seacycle@islandnet.com

Ritchey
Ritchey95@aol.com

Rivendell Bicycle Works
http://www.best.com/~bikiebob/rivendell
rivbici@aol.com

Santana
http://www.wsmith.com/veloling/santana
santanainc@aol.com

Schwinn
schwinboyz@aol.com

Softride
http://www.cyclelink.com/softride/
softride4u@aol.com

Specialized
http://www.specialized.com/bikes/

SpectrumCycles
spctrum@aol.com

Tango Tandems
rpjorgen@wheel.dcn.davis.ca.us

Terry Precision Bicycles
TPbike@aol.com

Ti Cycles
http://cyclery.com/ti_cycles/index.html

Totally Tandems
TTandems@aol.com

VooDoo Cycles
http://www.voodoo-cycles.com/
info@voodoo-cycles.com

Trek Bicycle
http://www.trekbikes.com

Waterford Precision Cycles
H20ford@aol.com

Wheeler Bicycles USA
http://www.interealm.com/p/bigmig/index.html
bigmig@nexus.interealm.com

Zipp
http://www.ipworld.com/MARKET/SPORTS/ZIPP/
HOMEPAGE.HTM

Bicycle Accessories/Components/Services

Avitar
http://www.accelerated.com/avitar

Airo-Series (helmets,beams)
http://www.ttinet.com/AiroSeries/
tom@ttisms.com

Basic Wheels
Basics@nether.net

Bebop Inc. (pedals, components)
mrbebop@aol.com

Bicycle Spare Tire Air & Sealant
http://www.metroguide.com/united

Bike News (reviews components)
bikenews@aol.com

Campagnolo USA
CampagUSA@aol.com

Cateye
CatEyeUSA@aol.com

Chosen Reflections (bicycle art)
http://www.primenet.com/~magazin
magazin@primenet.com

CyclArt Frame Painting
CyclArtist@aol.com

DuPont Lubes
http://www.lubricants.dupont.com/lubricants/
home.html

Equinox Ind., Inc (trailers)
http://www.efn.org/~equinox
equinox@efn.org

Full Speed Ahead
fsa@cmpedge.com

Gonzo Components USA
http://www.mindspring.com/~gonzousa/
index.html
gonzousa@mindspring.com

Greentyre Airless Tyres
http://www.greentyre.com/index.html

Info-Vid Outlet
http://branch.com/infovid/c330d.html

JB Professional Bike Refinishing
http://worldwise.com/jb/

Kooka Components
http://kooka.com

Load Llama (rack)
http://realinfo.com/llama.home.html

Lofox (helmets)
http://www.netaccess.on.ca/entrepr/idea/lofox
lofoxcan@maple.net

Look
http://www.adventuresports.com/asap/shops/
look.htm
veltec@aol.com

MIKLINK Bicycle Trailer System
http://www.londonmall.co.uk/miklink/

Miller Bicycle Restoration
http://www.bizpro.com/business/bizpro/
miller.html
mmiller@bizpro.com

Mountain Bikers Almanac
http://www.mbalmanac.com
mbalmanac@sierra.net

Naked International (MTB parts)
jon4est@aol.com

OnZa (pedals, components)
awtw@aol.com

Pace Bike Accessories
http://www.adventuresports.com/asap/shops/
pace.htm

Paul Component Engineering
pce@pinsight.com

Pedro's
androoh@aol.com
fina8@aol.com

Rak Sak
http://www.olympus.net/olympia/biz/jtb/
raksak.html
74771.2737@compuserve.com

Raqdaptour
raqdaptour@aol.com

Roadkill Products (BMX)
roadkillpr@aol.com

Roman Sports Graphics (posters)
http://www.accelerated.com/roman/

Sarkbars (aero bars, HR monitors)
sark47@delphi.com

Savage Bicycle Designs (saddles)
savagebike@aol.com

Seair Dynamics (trailers)
72302.2621@compuserve.com

Shock Works
shockworks@cmpedge.com

Slider Corp. (trailer hitch carriers)
http://www.slider.com
slidercorp@aol.com
slider@primenet.com

Solar Warning Light
http://www.valve.net/~esoteric/solar/warn.html

Spinergy
http://nsns.com/~spinergy
SpinergyXX@aol.com

Sportship (VeloCase)
http://www.holli.com/sportship
sports@holli.com

SRP
jughead10@aol.com

Studio 33 Cycling Artwork
(sculpture)
http://www.intersource.com/~studio33/
indexb.html

Sun Rims (aluminum rims/wheels)
sunrims@aol.com

Syncros
http://www.syncros.com/
art@alchemedia.net

Thule Bike Rack
http://www.sportsite.com:80/mac/allshop/sia/
thule/html/thule_hp.html
Thule1@aol.com

TNT Performance Products
TNTPerf@aol.com

Tortoise Products (Disc Defense
Security System)
http://www.maui.com/~perryman/TPI.html

Trek Wrench Force
splattski@aol.com

Tumbleweed Films
http://www.teleport.com/~tmblweed/TWF/
STT.html

Ultimate Bike Rack
http://realinfo.com/llama.home.html

Vittoria (tires)
http://www.vittoria.it/
info@vittoria.it

Vredestein Bicycle Tyres
http://neturl.nl/vredestein/

Zap Power Systems
http://nbn.nbn.com/inet/zap/
zap@nbn.com

Bicycle Sales/Classifieds

Atlantic Spoke Bicycles
http://www.vanet.com/atlantic
atlantic@vanet.com

Bicycle ShopView
http://www.interealm.com/infoview/
bikeshopview_web/mainpage/bikehome.html

Bike Nashbar
http://nashbar.com/
mail@nashbar.com

Bike Pedalers
http://www.bikeped.com/
bikeped@inetnebr.com

1-800-BIKE PRO Bicycle Parts
http://www.bikepro.com/
comments@bikepro.com
orders@bikepro.com
inquiries@bikepro.com

Bikesport
http://spider.netropolis.net/bikesport/
bikesport@netropolis.net

Bike Zone
http://www.iwsc.com/bikezone/index.html

Bike Trader
http://www.mind.net/biketrader

Broadway Bicycles
http://imsystem.com/bicycle/broadway/
index.html
BdwyBikes@aol.com

Budget Racer
http://www.mindspring.com/~budget/
budget.html

Cycle-Logic
http://cban.worldgate.edmonton.ab.ca/~cycle-
logic/
cycle@cban.com

Cycle Path Bike Shop
http://www.magicnet.net/cyclepath/
vax@magicnet.net

Cycle Sports
http://www.asisoft.com/cycle_sports_page/
cycle_sports_home_page.html
cyclesport@aol.com

Dean Ultimate Bicycles
http://www.omnibus.com/dean.html

Elegance Network Bicycles
http://www.netrunner.net/elegance/product/
bicycle/1.html

Encino Cyclery
http://members.aol.com/encinocycl/

EPages: Bicycle Classifieds
http://ep.com/s/gm/bik.html

Excel Sports Boulder
Excelsptsb@aol.com

Flying Cycle
bikedeals@aol.com

Futurecycles
http://www.demon.co.uk/history/cycles/
futurecycles.html

Gibraltar
http://gibikes.com/gib/
auto@gibikes.com

Habanero Cycles
Habby_Guy@aol.com

Hackensack Bicycle & Fitness
http://www.gearhead.com/shop.html

Harris Cyclery
http://www.tiac.net/users/captbike/index.htm
captbike@tiac.net

Internet Galleria Bike Store
http://intergal.com/Bikestor.hmtl

KMR Cycles
http://infoweb.magi.com/~kroberge/
kmrtop.html
kroberge@magi.com

Moto-Mark Cycles
MotoMark@delphi.com

Nytro
http://nytro.connectnet.com
nytro@connectnet.com

O'Neil's
508-792-2881 (BBS)

Physical Revolution
http://www.islandnet.com/~awilhelm/
revolution.html
awilhelm@islandnet.com

Rocky Mountain Bikes
http://www.rmii.com/rmbb/
rmbb@rmii.com

Rotrax Cycles
http://www.citivu.com/rc/rotrax/index.html
rotrax@citivu.com

Seaside Cycle
http://www.rscomm.com/adsports/seaside/
seaside_main.html
seaside@rscomm.com

Sportsworld
http://sportsworld.com/

Spring City Cycle
http://iquest.com:80/~topcycle/
topcycle@iquest.com

Start To Finish Online
http://www.stf.com/
#stfbikes (IRC channel)
comments@stf.com

Steve's Multisport
http://www.netaxs.com/~steves/
steves@netaxs.com

Supergo
fend13a@prodigy.com

Tandems East
TandemWiz@aol.com

Tandems, Limited
tandems@mindspring.com
tandems@viper.net

Together Tandems
TogTandems@aol.com

Tri Zombies
http://trizombies.com/trizombie

Velo Sportable Cycles
http://www.globalx.net/sportable/

Victorian Mountain Bike Centre
http://hyme.pcmicro.com.au/mtb
mtb@pcmicro.com.au

The Virtual Bike Shop
http://itlnet.com/media/bikeshop
jakespeare@aol.com

Wheel Works
http://www.wheelworks.com
support@wheelworks.com

Al Young's Bike and Ski
http://www.accelerated.com/al_young

YoYo Dynne Propulsion (broker)
meltonkc@halcyon.com

Bicycle Clothing

Armadillo
DILLOGEAR@aol.com

CheckNSee Network
http://ipages.prodigy.com/MA/stevedyk/
checknsee.html
CheckNSee@aol.com

Gortex
http://www.sportsite.goretex.com/
goreserv@aol.com

Lamson Design Shoes
http://www.fat-tire.com/catalog/lamson.html

Marmot Mountain Ltd.
http://www.marmot.com
info@marmot.com

Newsense
http://www.accelerated.com/newsense/

Pearl Izumi
http://www.sportsite.com/cedro/companies/
pearl/html/pearl_hp.html
pearlizumi@aol.com

Power Stroke
http://www.emf.net/~mwright
mwright@emf.net

Reebok
http://planetreebok.com/

RJ Cycle Wear (team apparel)
73014.2724@compuserve.com

Sidi
http://www.adventuresports.com/asap/shops/
sidi.htm
veltec@aol.com

SOHO Design
http://www.infomall.org/sohodesign/13.html
sohodes@westnet.com

Spokeswear
hutch626@aol.com

Ultima
http://www.adventuresports.com/asap/shops/
ultima.htm
veltec@aol.com

Training/Performance

Athlete's Diary
http://alumni.caltech.edu/~slp/tad.html
stevenscrk@aol.com

Bike Pro Cycling Software
http://www.he.net/~bikepro/
bikepro@dallas.net

Blue Pig (wheel building)
bluexpig@aol.com

Cycle Scribe, Cycle Graph
zanna@i2020.net

Do It Sports
http://www.doitsports.com

Endurance Plus
http://www.primenet.com/~buffed/
john@enduranceplus.com

Exercise Log Training Diary
http://fas-www.harvard.edu/~maurits/
ExerciseLog.html

Gatorade
http://gatorade.com/gatorade/entry.html

Al Kreitler Custom Rollers, Inc.
killertoo@aol.com

Performance Coaching (UK service)
http://ourworld.compuserve.com/homepages/
MShakeshaft

Polar Heart Rate Monitors
http://www.polar.fi/

PR*Nutrition
http://www.thegroup.net/prbar/prhome.htm
prbar@thegroup.net

Pro Trainer
http://www.indy.net/~pauld/HomePage.html

Racermate (CompuTrainer)
http://www.wsmith.com/veloling/racemate
racermate@aol.com

RadSport Technik (coaching)
http://users.aol.com/radsport/radsport.html
radsport@delphi.com

Rollerturbo (trainer)
http://pipex.net/people/simonm/rollerpg.htm

Sport Race Timing Program
becker@cdsnet.net

The Sports Source
http://s2.com/

Team Bauer (coaching)
http://www.uwm.edu/people/tjbrooks/bauer/
bauer.html

Train Right Software
http://iss.net/~train

Ultimate Performance National Cycling Camps (UPNCC)
http://www.abwam.com/upncc/
upncc@abwam.com

Ultracoach
http://s2.com/uc/index.html
ultracch@ix.netcom.com

Velo Tek Training Systems
velotek@aol.com

Travel/Tours

Adventuresports Institute
http://asi.gcc.cc.md.us/asi2/index.html
asiinfo@gcc.cc.md.us

Adventure Sports Online
http://www.adventuresports.com/

Adventurous Traveler Bookstore
http://www.gorp.com/atbook.htm
books@atbook.com

All-Inclusive Vacations
http://www.cts.com/~vacation/bike.html

America by Bicycle
http://www.abbike.com
info@abbike.com

American Dream Cruises (bike cruise)
ljmahar@aol.com

Australian Outbike Tours
jgroberg@rain.org

Bicycle Beano
http://www.zynet.co.uk/caius/local/beano/
bicycle.html

Big Bend Quarterly (B&B for mtb)
http://www.webcasting.com/bigbend/
bigbend@onramp.net

Big Twin Cycling Tours
http://www.meridian-com.com/bigtwin/
bigtwin.html
parcand@meridian-com.com

Blue Marble (European tours)
Blumarbl@pipeline.com

Company of Adventurers Wilderness Guides Ltd. (mtb tours)
http://www.worldtel.com/coa/home.html
coa@worldtel.com

Cycle America
http://www.mochinet.com/cycle

CYCLEVENTS
http://www.cyclevents.com/
biking@cyclevents.com

Cycling Adventures
http://www.travelsource.com/cycling/

Dirt Camp (MTB adventure camp)
http://www.dirtcamp.com/mtb
info@dirtcamp.com

Easy Rider Tours
http://www.rscomm.com/adsports/seaside/
seaside_main.html

Elpha Green Cottages (B&B on Sea to Sea Tour route)
http://georgia.ncl.ac.uk/BB/bicycling.html

Himalayan Travel
http://www.gorp.com/hmtravel.htm

Imagine Tours
http://vvv.com/imagine
imagine@vvv.com

Island Adventures: The Riau Islands
http://www.singnet.com.sg/~evanj/

Island Bicycles
islbike@aol.com

Kaibab's Mountain/Desert Bike Tours
http://www.netpub.com/kaibab

MacQueen's Bike Shop (tours)
http://www.peinet.pe.ca/PElhomepage/pei_biz/
macqueen/mcqtxt.html
biketour@bud.peinet.pe.ca

Nichols Expeditions
http://www.netpub.com/nichols/
Nictrips@aol.com

Rim Tours (Moab MTB)
rimtours@aol.com

Sunday River Ski Resort
http://sundayriver.com/WWW/sunday_river
skip@sundayriver.com

Travel Assistant Magazine
http://travelassist.com/

21st Century Adventures
http://www.10e-design.com/centadv/

Viking Adventure Tours of Greenland
http://www.sn.no/viking
viking@sn.no

Western Spirit Cycling
http://cyclery.com/western_spirit/index.html
WSCcycling@aol.com

White Meadow Press (Bed, Breakfast & Bike Series)
http://www.olympus.net/biz/windseye/bbb.html
bbb@windseye.com

Late-Breaking Sites

Because new cycling sites are coming online every day, we wanted to squeak in a few more recent resources.

American Center for Bicycle Registration
http://www.bikestar.com
(helps deter bicycle theft and return bikes to their owners)

Athlete's Heart Line
http://users.aol.com/ahline/
(tips for getting the most out of your heart rate monitor)

BMX On-Line
http://www.cityscape.co.uk/users/dv59
(Bob Shingleton brings a U.K. and international slant to BMX racing)

Fixed Gear Fever
http://www.earthlink.net/~durer/fgf/
(Durer Shomer's excellent Online Journal of Bicycle Track Racing)

Go Ride!
http://www.goride.com
(Biker Dave provides cycling routes, history, links, and more)

Mountain Bike!
http://home.sol.no/geirvb/
(Geir Bjørndalen's well-organized off-road site)

Mountain Biking FAQ
http://www.srv.ualberta.ca/~vccheng/cycling.html
(Vincent Cheng also offers tips for commuting and winter riding)

Outdoor Resources Online: Mountain Biking
http://www.azstarnet.com/~goclimb/mtbhome.html
(Mark Fleming's comprehensive index to mountain biking resources)

Pedalling Preacher's Cycle Training
http://www.ozemail.com.au/~tcdc/tp.html
(Terry Churchill preaches the good news of training)

The Treehouse
http://users.aol.com/mlkienholz
(home of *Cycling in Cyberspace* online)

Your Biking Accident
http://www.duke.usa.usask.ca/~yeo/your_accident.html
(Chris Yeo's thoughtfully designed database of cycling accidents)

Index

regional resources 50, 57, 58, 60, 112, 117
repair. *See* maintenance
Ritchey, Tom 91, 92

S

safety 29, 52, 80, 81, 107
Scott, Dave 91
search engine 112, 114, 116
shareware 15
slow connections 136–137
Snell Memorial Foundation 84, *86*
software 15, 19, 49, 64, 66, 110
    Athlete's Diary 97
    communications 12, 16, 19
    Exercise Log 99
    GIF viewer 26
    Internet 33
    IRC 43
    macros 15
    Pro Trainer 102
    QWK utility 19
    shareware 15
    Software Exchange 27
    spoke length calculator 25, 83, 84
    training (commercial) 152
    training log 25, 51, 83, 97, 99, 102, 108
    Velocipede 51
    virus 15, 42
specifications. *See* companies
sports medicine. *See* medical information
sports psychology 65, 102
stage races 64, 71–72
Stolen Bike Registry 84
stretching 100, 102
subject line 134
system operator (sysop) 11, 19

T

Tandem Club of America 78
tandems 77, 78, 83, 94, 109, 112, 113
Team Internet *40, 69*
team rosters 64, 67, 111, 112, 114
Team Working Title *70*
Tech Tips *39,* 85
technical tips 24, 25, 52, 81, 85, 89, 90, 91, 92, 94. *See also* maintenance
telnet 43
threads 37, 132–133
time trial 64
Tomac, John 92
Tour de France 24, 64, 67, 70, 72, 91, 93, 96, 114

Tour DuPont 72
Tour of China 72
touring 23, 48, 51, 73, 89, 113, 155
tours 28, 31, 49, 50, 53, 78, 93, 110, 117, 153
track 66, 89, 155
trails 58, 60, 61, 83, 95
training 24, 25, 49, 51, 62, 64, 65, 66, 78, 90, 91, 93, 95, 97, 98, 100, 102, 103, 155
Travel Guide 117
triathlon 57, 77, 87, 91, 95, 98, 105–108

U

U.S. Bicycling Hall of Fame 53
U.S. Congress 83
UltraMarathon Cycling Association 113
unicycling 75, 78
United States Cycling Federation (USCF) 26, 30, 42, 65, 70, 138, 155
universal resource locator (URL) 41, 136, 137

V

VeloNet 45–47, 67, 69, 143–146
Veronica 38
video 62, 70, 91
virus 15, 42
Vuelta a España 72

W

weather 48, 51, 57, 60, 93, 105, 113, 130
Web browser 39, 40–41, 42, 44
WebCrawler *114,* 138, 147
Wide Area Information Server (WAIS) 39
winter cycling *85*
WOMBATS 61
women 24, 25, 26, 61, 64, 70, 98, 109, 111
World Health Organization 86
World Wide Web (WWW) 40–41, 137
WWW Sports Page 97

Y

Yahoo! *104,* 116, 147
Young, Roger 25

Z

Zen and the Art of the Internet 32
Zmodem 16

Other Titles Available from Bicycle Books

Title	Author	US Price
All Terrain Biking	Jim Zarka	$7.95
The Backroads of Holland	Helen Colijn	$12.95
The Bicycle Commuting Book	Rob van der Plas	$7.95
The Bicycle Fitness Book	Rob van der Plas	$7.95
The Bicycle Repair Book	Rob van der Plas	$9.95
Bicycle Repair Step by Step (color)*	Rob van der Plas	$14.95
Bicycle Technology	Rob van der Plas	$16.95
Bicycle Touring International	Kameel Nasr	$18.95
The Bicycle Touring Manual	Rob van der Plas	$16.95
Bicycling Fuel	Richard Rafoth, M.D.	$9.95
Cycling Canada	John Smith	$12.95
Cycling in Cyberspace	Kienholz & Pawlak	$14.95
Cycling Europe	Nadine Slavinski	$12.95
Cycling France	Jerry Simpson	$12.95
Cycling Great Britain	Hughes & Cleary	$14.95
Cycling Kenya	Kathleen Bennett	$12.95
Cycling the Mediterranean	Kameel Nasr	$14.95
Cycling the San Francisco Bay Area	Carol O'Hare	$12.95
Cycling the U.S. Parks	Jim Clark	$12.95
In High Gear (hardcover)	Samuel Abt	$21.95
The High Performance Heart	Maffetone & Mantell	$10.95
The Mountain Bike Book	Rob van der Plas	$10.95
Mountain Bike Maintenance (color)	Rob van der Plas	$10.95
Mountain Bikes: Maint. & Repair*	Stevenson & Richards	$22.50
Mountain Bike Racing (hardcover)*	Burney & Gould	$22.50
Mountain Biking the National Parks	Jim Clark	$12.95
The New Bike Book	Jim Langley	$4.95
Roadside Bicycle Repairs	Rob van der Plas	$7.95
Tour of the Forest Bike Race (color)	H.E. Thomson	$9.95
Cycle History – 4th International Conference Proceedings (hardcover)		$30.00
Cycle History – 5th International Conference Proceedings (hardcover)		$45.00

Buy our books at your local book store or bike shop.

If you have difficulty obtaining our books elsewhere, we will be pleased to supply them by mail, but we must add $2.50 postage and handling, or $3.50 for priority mail (and California Sales Tax if mailed to a California address). Prepayment by check or credit card must be included.

Bicycle Books, Inc.
1282 – 7th Avenue
San Francisco, CA 94122
Tel.   (415) 665-8214
FAX   (415) 753-8572

In Britain: Bicycle Books
463 Ashley Road
Poole, Dorset BH14 0AX
Tel.   (01202) 71 53 49
FAX   (01202) 73 61 91

* Books marked thus not available from Bicycle Books in the U.K.